The Mask She Wore

THE REBIRTH

MADELINE O. AGOBA

© **Copyright 2025 Madeline O. Agoba**

All rights reserved.

Paperback ISBN 978-1-970522-02-0

No portion of this book may be reproduced, stored in a retrieval system or transmitted in any form or by any means, electronic, mechanical, photocopy, recording, scanning or other, except for brief quotations in critical reviews or articles, without the written permission of the author.

DEDICATION

To my Beloved, my Lord, at whose feet I find myself. In Your presence, I am remade, healed, and continually transformed. My Savior, my Refuge, my Strength, this work is birthed from Your grace, Your patience, and Your love.

ACKNOWLEDGMENTS

To my husband, who stood by me, even when he did not know the full weight I carried behind my smile. You held space for me without knowing the battles behind the mask. You cried with me and wondered aloud how I bore it all after you found out. Your love has been a steady echo of grace.

To my children, whose innocence, laughter, and unconditional love reminded me daily that I was never too broken to be loved. You never judged me, even when I stumbled. You simply stayed, and that has been a song of healing I will forever sing.

To my mother and siblings, thank you for loving me in the silent seasons, when words were few but prayers spoke louder.

And to the community of friends whose intercessions became air when I could no longer breathe hope, thank you.

To **The Esther Company**, the gatekeepers who prayed with me, for me, and sometimes carried me when I could not stand. You taught me that sisterhood isn't perfect, but it is sacred.

To **The Threshing Floor**, that quiet place of surrender, where masks fell and raw prayers rose. You helped me learn that being broken before God is not weakness but the beginning of strength.

To the pastors who passed the baton into my spirit:

- Pastor Chris Oyakhilome, who laid the foundation of Christ-consciousness in my heart and taught me the necessity of anchoring my identity in Him.
- Bishop David Oyedepo, who stirred faith into my bones and emphasized the sacred discipline of recording every encounter with God, a reminder that accountability is worship.
- Pastor Jentezen Franklin, whose raw and piercing sermons helped me peel back the layers I didn't even know I had, starting the long journey of unveiling.

You each deposited something eternal in me, unknowingly, across the seasons of my life, and I am grateful beyond words.
Thank you for being part of the journey.

Author's Note

In some places, debt is just a number. It lives on spreadsheets, in bank statements, and on payment plans. It's an inconvenience, sometimes even a strategy.

But where I come from, debt is not that simple.

Debt is a whisper that travels faster than truth.
It's a stain on your name, even when your hands are clean.
It's the glance that lingers too long when your name is mentioned.
It's the silent verdict that says, "You have failed."

In my world, debt doesn't just affect your wallet; it seeps into your faith. It questions your prayers. It makes you second-guess the God you once trusted. It presses you into corners where hope feels like a foreign language.

However, in church, the one place where a mask should fall, debt is often the topic no one wants to touch. We preach about prosperity, faith, and abundance, but we bury conversations about lack, shame, and the quiet despair of unpaid bills. Many suffer in the pews with smiles on their faces, often carrying what their testimonies never name.

So I wore a mask. A strong woman's smile over a trembling soul. Not because I loved pretending, but because vulnerability, in a culture where shame speaks louder than grace, felt too dangerous.

This book is not about shame. It's about the God who meets us in the whispers, in the corners, and even behind the masks. The One who calls us out, not to expose us, but to restore us.

My story isn't finished. I'm still a work in progress. God is not done with me yet.

Perhaps, somewhere in these pages, my cracks might give you the courage to remove your own mask also.

A Psalm To My Beloved

To my Beloved,
My Lord, my Anchor,
The Keeper of every sigh and every stumble
To the One who sat with me in silence when words failed,
Who held me through the nights the tears wouldn't stop,
Who whispered when I could no longer pray,
And who kept calling me closer, even when I hid behind my mask.
To the Lover of my soul,
Whose gaze never flinched at my brokenness,
Whose mercy met me in the secret places I never dared to show anyone,
Whose presence became the safest place I've ever known.
To the One who peeled back every layer gently,
Who watched me shatter and still stayed,
Who made beauty from what I called shame,
And who taught me that I could breathe again,
not because I was strong,
But because He is.
This is for You.
Every word. Every story. Every sacred hush.
I am still at Your feet, still becoming,
Still learning to live unveiled.
And I wouldn't want it any other way.
Forever Yours,
The One You Found Behind the Mask

PREFACE

I wrote this with trembling fingers and a full heart, not because I had all the answers, but because I also wore a mask that fit so snugly. It almost became my skin. I hid behind strength and laughed through the pain. I served with an aching emptiness, and when my mask finally slipped, I feared I'd fall apart.

It was there, in that vulnerable space, that I met Him.

This devotional is not just for the perfect or the poised. It's for the ones whose strength is weakened. The woman who still smiles while breaking. For the man drowning in "enough." For the one who is weary of pretending.

It is for you.

Let every story awaken you to the beauty of being fully seen. Let every reflection draw you closer to the God who calls you out from behind the veil.

There is healing on the other side of your honesty, and I pray, with every word, that you'll find the courage to meet Him there.

Don't be mistaken. She is still healing, peeling off the layers, learning, and on the altar. She is still a work in progress.

This book is not the voice of the arrived. It's the voice of the becoming.

Welcome to The Mask She Wore: The Rebirth, where masks fall and mercy finds us.

Yours Sincerely,
Madeline O. Agoba

THE FIRST OF MANY LAYERS

I can't quite tell you when I put it on.
Maybe it wasn't a moment at all, but a slow, silent folding-in.
A thousand tiny choices stitched together like lace.
Invisible at first, until it wasn't.

Was it when I learned that being the "good child" earned nods of approval and left less room for disappointment?
Or when I caught the tired look in my parents' eyes, and something inside me decided, without instruction, that I would not be another weight on their already burdened backs?

Maybe it was when I realized that silence was safer than need.
That composure was currency.
That girls who didn't ask for much were the ones called *strong*.

Or perhaps, it began even deeper.
In the undercurrents of a culture that demands so much and gives so little to the girl child, especially the first daughter.
Where you are born with expectations heavier than your own name.
Where you are taught to bend before you know how to stand.
First the dutiful daughter, then the dependable sister and the tireless wife.
Always shaping yourself around others, until you forget the shape of your own soul.
No one ever asked what I wanted to be perfect *for*.
Only that I be perfect *to*.

I don't remember the first time I put the mask on.
But I remember how it hugged my face like a second skin.
How the world clapped for her; this version of me who never flinched or faltered.

She was everything they needed.
And nothing I truly was.

The mask told them I was fine. That I had it all together. That I could carry it *all*.
And for a long time, I did.
Until I couldn't.

Until the cracks began. Tiny. Hairline. Quiet.
Until the ache leaked through the seams.
Until one day, the mask didn't fall; it simply, slipped.
And I didn't have the strength to fix it.

This devotional was born in that holy unraveling.
Where I stopped pretending to be strong long enough to be *seen*.
Where grace whispered, "You don't have to earn being held."
Where the pieces I thought disqualified me became the very place God met me.
So, no, I cannot tell you the day I put it on.
But I remember the weight of it.
And I can tell you, with trembling clarity,
What it felt like the day the mask began to fall.

Are you ready to get yours off?

Are you even aware you may be crumbling under a mask too?

What have you given up just to be seen, heard and stay relevant?

Let's take a ride to your unveiling right in the pages of this devotional.

Shall we?

INTERLUDE: THE THORN AND THE MASK

We all have something we pray away.

A debt that won't disappear, weaknesses that won't let up, habits we hate and silence that echoes back nothing.

Paul called his *a thorn*. He pleaded for it to leave three times. And God's reply? *"My grace is sufficient for you. My power is made perfect in weakness."* 2Corinthians 12:9. (KJV).

It wasn't the answer Paul wanted. But it was the one his soul needed.

That answer still wrecks us today. Because we've been taught to equate power with performance. Strength with perfection. Healing with disappearance. We don't know how to carry a thorn *and* still believe we're loved.

So we perform. We pretend. We hide.

We wear the mask.

"I'm fine," we say, when the debt suffocates.
"I'm good," we whisper, while silently falling apart.
"Blessed and highly favored," we declare, while wondering why God feels so far.
"It is well," we boldly say with wide grins while the well of pain in our hearts seems so deep.

And now, in a world that glamorizes curated truth, a new lie has emerged. "Fake it till you make it."
But what if faking it is the very thing keeping you from healing?

What if the real breakthrough begins not in pretending but in pausing?

Because the truth is: the devil is a master deceiver. He wore a mask in Eden, he wore one in the wilderness, and he's still whispering in your ear, "Just hide it better."

But God,
God doesn't shame you for your thorn.
He doesn't leave because you're tired.
He doesn't turn away from the wounds you've bandaged for too long.

He leans in.
And He calls you by name.

So maybe the thorn didn't leave because the grace never would.
Maybe the weakness stayed because strength was never meant to look like perfection.
Maybe Paul wasn't less anointed with the thorn but more honest. More real. More free.

And maybe, so are you.

If you've been wearing a mask to survive the silence, to outrun the shame, or to hide the thorn, this is your invitation.

Come, sit in the hush!

Let the journey begin.

DAY 1

THE MASK SHE WORE

SCRIPTURES

"Though the mountains be shaken and the hills be removed, yet my unfailing love for you will not be shaken nor my covenant of peace be removed," says the Lord, who has compassion on you."
- **Isaiah 54:10. (NIV).**

"You have searched me, Lord, and you know me. You know when I sit and when I rise; you perceive my thoughts from afar."
- **Psalm 139:1–2. (NIV).**

STORY REFLECTION: THE QUIET UNDOING

The mask was a shield, a well-worn carefully practiced expression of strength. She wore it so convincingly that even those closest to her never saw beneath it. On the outside, she looked unshakable: a pillar of faith, hope, and wisdom. But inside, she was fraying.

She had weathered many storms:

- The loss of her father left her adrift in grief.
- Her husband's illness quietly drained her, night after night, as she poured from a cup that rarely got refilled.
- Friends who once called her "sister" betrayed her, unsettled by the glimpse of where she was headed.
- Debt pressed against her chest like a weight she couldn't throw off.

She was walking through fog, holding hands with uncertainty, unsure of what tomorrow would bring. But she had to keep going. People looked up to her, leaned on her and called her "strong."

So, she said nothing. She just took in all the accolades.

Because if they really knew, if they saw beneath the surface, would their love shift? Would their respect crumble? To them, she was the strong one, the counsellor and the steady voice when their own worlds caved in. They couldn't see her any less.

- She was a mother, steadfast, pouring into her children's dreams, sacrificing sleep and sanity
- A wife gently wiping her husband's brow, whispering hope into his weariness even when her own hands trembled.
- An employee showing up daily to a job that drained her soul because quitting wasn't an option.
- A faithful churchgoer wearing her Sunday best and lifting her hands even when her heart felt hollow.
- An evangelist preaching with fire, pointing others to the Light even as her own flame flickered.
- A daughter checking on her frail mother.
- A sister holding the family thread with phone calls, visits, and prayers.

She was everything to everyone.

But inside, she was becoming nothing to herself.

But how could she admit she was drowning?

That she was dying inside?

She wore the mask not for vanity but for survival. Smiles stitched over pain. Strength concealing shame. No one saw the mounting debt. No one heard the midnight prayers or the silence after another unanswered call for help. She buried her truth under sleepless nights and anxious whispers into pillows.

It was safer to stay silent than risk losing the love she desperately needed. She wore the mask for so long that she forgot what her real face looked like.

But even in her hiding, **He was there.**

One evening, in the stillness between prayer and tears, she heard it. A voice. Gentle. Familiar. Steady.

"Let Me in."

Her heart clenched. The mask cracked. Could it be? Was this the One who knew the garden behind her walls and loved her still?

There He was, **Love Himself.** Not asking her to explain. Not waiting for her to clean up the mess. Just knocking. Just calling. Just waiting to be let in.

DEVOTIONAL THOUGHT

God doesn't love the mask.
He loves you.

The real you.
The overwhelmed you.
The exhausted, tear-streaked, worn-out you that no one else sees.

And He is knocking, not to shame you, but to heal you.

In Song of Solomon 4:16, the bride invites her Beloved into her garden. But before the invitation came, there was preparation. Waiting. Longing. The Beloved was never far; He had always been near.

The same is true with the Father.

He's not afraid of your mess. He's not intimidated by your silence, debts, and doubts. He longs for you. And like Hosea loved Gomer, despite her wanderings, God's love chases, covers, and cleanses.

He comes to tear down walls and rebuild identity.
To unmask shame and clothe you in dignity.
To turn your weary soul into a well-watered garden again.

INTERACTIVE REFLECTION

We all wear masks, some obvious, some hidden.
1. What mask have you been wearing lately?
- The mask of "I'm fine"?
- The mask of spiritual performance while bleeding inside?
2. What would it look like to let Him into your pain, not just your performance?

QUESTION AND ANSWER

Q: What do you fear people would say if they really knew what you're dealing with or if they found out the story behind your glory?

A: God already knows. Not the curated version, the real you. And yet, **He stays**.

He doesn't flinch at the debt, doubt, or the disappointment.

He isn't looking for performance, just permission.

When you finally drop the mask, you'll realize that He was never waiting for your perfection. He was waiting for your surrender.

SCRIPTURE FOR MEDITATION

"See, I have taken away your sins, and now I am giving you these fine new clothes............" - **Zechariah 3:1-7 (NLT)**.

REFLECTIVE PROMPTS

- Where do you feel accused or ashamed?
- What "filthy garment" or mask have you been hiding behind?
- Are you willing to let God remove it and clothe you in what He sees fit?
- Are you ready to come out with the mess behind your glory?

NOTES FROM MY JOURNAL

I didn't even know when I started wearing it.

Maybe it was after the betrayal,
Maybe it was when I had to be strong for everyone else…
Maybe it was when I realized that vulnerability felt too expensive.

What I do know is I perfected it.
That smile. That faith talk. That "I'm fine" That "it is well" nod even when my chest was burning with anxiety.

But I wasn't fine.

I remember crying in the bathroom and fixing my makeup before heading back out to a room full of people who needed me.
I remember praying for others and wondering if God still remembered me.
I remember encouraging someone with verses I hadn't felt in my own bones in a long time.

There was a night I whispered, *"God, are You still here?"*
And I didn't hear the faintest sigh or thunder. I didn't get a miracle. But I felt a hush.
A holy hush.
As if love wrapped a blanket around my worn-out soul and whispered, *"I never left."*

That night, the mask cracked

And for the first time in a long time, I didn't feel ashamed. I felt seen.

MY REFLECTION NOTES

(Use this space to write your thoughts, prayers, or what stood out to you today.)

_____

_____

_____

_____

_____

Date: _____

Thoughts & Impressions

_____

_____

_____

_____

_____

PRAYER

Father,

I've worn many masks: some to protect, some to survive.

But You see me. Every broken piece. Every mounting debt. Every unpaid bill. Every silent prayer.

And still, You love me.

Today, I lay the mask down.

Come into my garden, into the places I've kept hidden, and call them beautiful again.

You are Jehovah-Nissi, my banner of victory, even when I feel defeated.

Amen.

DAY 2

THE MIRROR LIED

SCRIPTURE:

"For now we see only a reflection as in a mirror; then we shall see face to face. Now I know in part; then I shall know fully, even as I am fully known."
- 1 Corinthians 13:12 (NIV).

STORY REFLECTION: THE SILENT SHATTER

The mirror was older than her. A rectangular frame with dulled edges, mounted to a wall that had seen three generations of women adjust their faces before stepping into the world.

She had grown up watching her mother in front of that mirror, pinning headscarves, pressing powder into her cheekbones, holding in tears with a posture of pride. Strength, she learned early, had a look. It wasn't soft or trembling. It stood tall, silent, sharp-eyed and dignified, even while breaking.

So, she mimicked it.

She was eight the first time she stood on a stool to reach her reflection. Her lips trembled from holding in a cry. Her hair had been pulled too tight, and school had been unkind. She looked at the mirror, wiped her tears, and whispered, "Be strong." No one taught her that. She just, knew.

By eighteen, she could smile on cue, laugh without joy, and make pain look like poetry. The mirror was no longer just glass; it was a rehearsal space, a disguise lab, a sanctuary where she crafted the woman she believed the world could tolerate. One that didn't bleed too much. One that didn't ask for anything.

Then came the year everything unraveled.

It began slowly, with small betrayals. Friends who turned away. A dream that died in her hands before it even had a name. The ache in her chest started as a whisper, then became a scream she couldn't silence. But still, each morning, she stood before the mirror; adjusted her posture, lifted her chin and smiled.

Until one day, she couldn't.

That morning, the mirror looked foreign. Her face was familiar, but her eyes startled her. They were vacant, tired and hunted.

And then it happened, without warning, without ceremony. Another layer of mask cracked.

Not with a sob or a scream, but with a question:

"Who are you?"

It came from deep inside, the part of her that had waited years to be heard. She sank to the floor, back against the wall, and wept. Not the elegant kind. The kind that shakes your body and breaks your pride.

And for the first time, she didn't rush to fix it.

She let the tears fall. She let the truth rise.

And in that sacred undoing, she felt it, a Presence. Not condemning. Not cold. But near.

A whisper:

"I see you. I always have."

The mirror didn't lie. It simply never showed the whole story. But God did.

He saw the little girl who learned silence as survival.
The teenager who performed strength.
The woman who nearly disappeared beneath the image she wore.

He saw it all and loved her still.

DEVOTIONAL THOUGHT

There comes a time in every journey when the masks we've worn become too heavy. When performance exhausts us and the mirror no longer cooperates with the lie.

God is not waiting for you to get it all together before He sees you. He's been watching from the beginning. Not the rehearsed version, but the raw, beautiful, bruised truth of who you are.

He doesn't flinch.
He doesn't turn away.
He leans in.

Where the world demands performance, He offers presence.
Where the mirror reflects a part, He reveals the whole.
And where shame tries to silence, He speaks love louder.

Let the mask fall.
Let the truth breathe.
Let Him show you who you've been all along.

INTERACTIVE REFLECTION

1. Have you ever built your life around an image just to survive?
2. Have you ever felt the hollow ache of being known only for your strength, not your softness?
3. What would it look like to let God meet the version of you that you've hidden, even from yourself?

QUESTION AND ANSWER

Q: What was behind my mask that even I was afraid to confront?

A: A tender soul, hungry to be seen. A story too sacred for performance. A truth too weighty to carry alone.

SCRIPTURES FOR MEDITATION

- *"The Lord is close to the brokenhearted and saves those who are crushed in spirit."* - **Psalm 34:18. (NIV).**
- *"Nothing in all creation is hidden from God's sight."* - **Hebrews 4:13. (NIV).**
- *"People look at the outward appearance, but the Lord looks at the heart."* - **1 Samuel 16:7. (NIV).**

REFLECTIVE PROMPTS

- What do I believe I must hide to be loved or accepted?
- Where did I first learn that my softness was a liability?
- What do I hear when God says, "I see you"?
- If I stop rehearsing, what truth might finally be free to speak?

NOTES FROM MY JOURNAL

Wearing these masks became second nature, a silent companion I didn't notice until they started to feel heavy.

It carried the weight of unseen battles and quiet sacrifices no one applauded.

The masks held back the storm inside while I showed up, day after day, for everyone else.

I mastered the art of speaking courage while feeling broken, and offering prayers when my own hope flickered dimly.

I watched myself move through rooms filled with people who needed me, even when I was running on empty.

There were moments when exhaustion whispered to me, begging me to let go, but the masks stayed firmly in place.

Until one night, when silence was deeper than usual, and my heart couldn't keep pretending.

In that sacred stillness, I felt something shift, not a loud awakening, but a gentle unraveling.

A subtle invitation to be real, to be vulnerable, to let the mask fall without fear.

It was the beginning of freedom, a quiet breaking open that promised healing beyond the facade.

MY REFLECTION NOTES

(Use this space to write your thoughts, prayers, or what stood out to you today.)

_____

_____

_____

_____

_____

Date: _____

Thoughts & Impressions

_____

_____

_____

_____

_____

PRAYER

Jesus,

I've worn these masks for so long. I've hidden my doubts, fears, and exhaustion.
But You see me. And You don't flinch.

I thought I had to be strong to stay loved.
But when I let each mask fall, I found You closer than ever.

Thank You for not turning away.
Thank You for calling me Yours even in my mess.

Teach me to rest in Your nearness and trust that I don't need to perform to be pursued.

Let my heart remember this truth:
I am fully seen.
And fully loved.

Amen.

DAY 3

WHERE HEALING BEGINS

SCRIPTURES

"He brought me to the banqueting house, and his banner over me was love."
- **Songs of Solomon 2:4. (NKJV).**

"He heals the brokenhearted and binds up their wounds."
- **Psalm 147:3. (NKJV).**

STORY REFLECTION: HEALING BEGINS WHEN WE STOP HIDING

As each layer of mask fell and the tears came, she waited.

Waited for rejection.
For judgment.
For the silence that usually follows truth.

She expected Him to turn away like others had when she'd let them see too much.
She braced herself for the sting of disappointment or pity.
She feared she had ruined everything with her honesty.

But instead, she felt a hand.

Not cold or distant.
Not rushed or intrusive.
But steady.
Warm.
Sure.

A hand that reached into the deep soil of her soul.

And He began to tend her garden.
He didn't hurry. He didn't say, *"You should be over this by now."*
He didn't ask for explanations or timelines.

He just stayed.
He poured mercy into the dry, cracked ground of her heart.

He loosened the roots of bitterness, gently pulling up the lies that had grown like weeds.
He watered the places she had long abandoned.
He tended to her soul with quiet faithfulness.

Then He spoke, not loudly, but clearly.
Words that fell like rain on dry land:

"Live."
"Rest."
"You are Mine."

And at that moment, something shifted.

No applause. No spotlight.
Just quiet growth.

She was no longer trying to prove her worth.
No longer performing for affection.
She simply was **loved**, **rooted**, and at **home**.

Healing didn't begin with fixing everything.
It began by being held.

Her Maker was in charge now.

DEVOTIONAL THOUGHT

God rarely enters our pain with thunder.
More often, He comes like a Gardener, quiet, intentional, patient.

He doesn't shame you into healing.
He *stays* until you're ready to bloom.

In **Songs of Solomon**, the Beloved brings her into the banqueting house and marks her with love, not judgment, not shame, not performance. Just absolute **Love.**

God doesn't rush your process.
Even in your mess.
Even in the in-between.

He will keep tending until every wilted place becomes a bloom.

INTERACTIVE REFLECTION

1. Have you ever felt pressure to "clean yourself up" before coming to God?
2. What would it look like to believe that He is patient with your healing?
3. Where in your soul do you sense Him beginning to tend to your garden again?

QUESTION AND ANSWER

Q: What if I still feel broken even after I've "given it to God"?

A: Healing is rarely instant.

It's a process, and God is not in a hurry.

His presence is not proof of your perfection; it's a promise of His commitment.

Let the healing be slow. Let Him determine the pace.

Let it be sacred.

SCRIPTURE FOR MEDITATION:

"He brought me to the banqueting house, and his banner over me was love."
- **Songs of Solomon 2:4 (ESV).**

REFLECTIVE PROMPTS:

- Sit still for five minutes today and imagine God tending to your heart like a garden.
- What part of your soul needs watering?
- Write a letter to God describing the "weeds" you're afraid He'll see.

Then ask Him to show you how He sees those places instead.

NOTES FROM MY JOURNAL

After the mask fell and the tears dried on my cheeks, I sat in silence, waiting.
Waiting for the backlash.
For the ache of being "too much" for someone again.
I was bracing for rejection, even from God.

But that's not what I found.
I found Him waiting too, not to rebuke, but to remain.
Not to point out how messy I was, but to *enter the mess with me*.

I didn't hear a sermon.
I didn't get a "to-do" list to clean myself up.
I just felt it: a steady hand, holding me when I didn't even know I needed holding.

He didn't rush me.
He didn't flinch at the tangled weeds of my heart.
He just *gardened* me.

Slowly. Gently.

With the patience I never gave myself.

And then He said something I didn't know I was longing to hear: "Live."

It wasn't a command.

It was an invitation.

To exhale.

To be.

To stop performing and simply rest in being *His*.

That was the beginning of my healing.

Not the end of my problems.

But the end of hiding.

MY REFLECTION NOTES

(Use this space to write your thoughts, prayers, or what stood out to you today.)

_____

_____

_____

_____

_____

Date: _____

Thoughts & Impressions

_____

_____

_____

_____

PRAYER

Father,

Thank You for not rushing me.
For not turning away when I'm messy, tired, or unfinished.

Thank You for staying in the stillness, the pain, and the process.
Thank You for not being put off by the debts I carry, emotional, financial, spiritual.

Teach me to trust the pace of Your love.
Water the garden of my heart.
Help me surrender to the gentle hands that tend my soul.

Let me bloom quietly, fully, with You.

Amen.

DAY 4

SHE ALMOST PUT IT BACK ON

SCRIPTURES

"Who is this coming up from the wilderness leaning on her beloved?"
- **Songs of Solomon 8:5a. (NKJV).**

*"Fear not, for I have redeemed you;
I have called you by name, you are mine."*
- **Isaiah 43:1b. (NKJV).**

STORY REFLECTION: NOWHERE TO HIDE

She was healing.
Really healing.
She could feel it in the way she breathed easier.
In how she didn't flinch as often.
In how she cried less when she prayed and sometimes, she even smiled.

The heaviness that once lived in her chest had started lifting like early morning fog.
She no longer woke up dreading the day.
The voices that once screamed shame now only whispered.

But healing doesn't mean you forget how to break.

So, when they said it, that thing, that comment, that backhanded praise that cut like a curse, something in her *shifted*.

She wasn't prepared for it.
She thought she had moved past that version of herself.
But just like that, the panic rose in her throat like wildfire.

All those old instincts came rushing back:

- *Smile even though you're hurting.*
- *Say you're fine even though you're unraveling.*
- *Control the situation before someone controls the narrative about you.*

And there it was, the mask. Right where she left it.
She hadn't worn it in a while, but it was still there. Still intact. Still available.

She reached for it almost by reflex.
Because the truth?
The mask still felt like comfort.
It still felt like safety.

But this time, she paused.

Right there, between breath and reaction, she *heard* Him.
Not audibly. But unmistakably.

"You don't need it anymore."

Her hand trembled.
She could feel her soul torn between what was and what could be.
Between hiding again or trusting what she had started to believe:

That she was lovable. Without the mask.
That she was chosen. Even when she wasn't polished.
That she was safe. Even when she wasn't silent.

So instead of disappearing into the old version of herself, she did the scariest, most holy thing.

She leaned.

Not on her performance.
Not on her need to be strong.
Not even on her healing.

She leaned on the One who loved her when she was broken and loves her still.

DEVOTIONAL THOUGHT

Healing isn't linear. It's layered.
And sometimes, when old wounds are triggered, we're tempted to revert.

To return to the mask.
To the silence.
To the illusion of control.

But if healing has taught us anything, it's this:
We are not who we used to be.

Yes, the mask is still within reach, so is the Voice.
The Voice that calls you Beloved.
That reminds you who you are.
That invites you to **lean**, not hide.

In **Song of Solomon 8:5**, the bride emerges from the wilderness, but she's not standing tall and fierce.
She's **leaning**.

That's the posture of the healed:
Not independent. Not flawless. But leaning.

Leaning on Love.
Leaning on Grace.
Leaning on the One who saw them through the wilderness.

INTERACTIVE REFLECTION

1. What triggers make you want to retreat behind old masks?
2. Are there situations or people that tempt you to pretend or perform again?

3. What would it look like to **lean** instead of retreat?

QUESTION AND ANSWER

Q: What if I still feel safer behind the mask sometimes?

A: That's OK.

God doesn't shame you for that instinct.
He simply invites you to pause and **lean instead**.

To remember: You are no longer hiding in the wilderness.
You're walking out of it, **leaning on your Beloved**.

SCRIPTURE FOR MEDITATION:

> *"You are altogether beautiful, my love; there is no flaw in you."*
> - **Songs of Solomon 4:7. (ESV).**

REFLECTIVE PROMPTS:

- What mask are you tempted to wear when you feel triggered?
- What does "leaning" look like for you in real life: prayer, silence, asking for help, journaling?

NOTES FROM MY JOURNAL

I didn't expect to be triggered.
I thought I was past that place, one where a single sentence could shake me.
But healing is funny like that… it's not a straight line.
It's a holy ground paved with memories, and some days, old echoes feel fresh again.

The moment I heard their words, I felt it.
That old, familiar urge to shrink, to edit myself, to reach for the mask that once protected me.

It was right there.
So easy to slip back into.
It still *fit*.

And for a second, I almost did it.
I almost disappeared into her again, the version of me that always smiled, stayed quiet, and carried the weight.

But right in the tug of it, He whispered:
"You don't need it anymore."

I froze.
Could I really believe that?
Could I trust that who I am, unfiltered, unguarded, is enough?

It was terrifying.
But I leaned into that whisper.
I didn't perform. I didn't pretend.
I just *breathed* as myself.
No edits. No masks. Just trust.

Healing isn't about becoming invincible.
It's about becoming *true*.
And today, I chose truth over comfort.

MY REFLECTION NOTES

(Use this space to write your thoughts, prayers, or what stood out to you today.)

_____
_____
_____
_____
_____

Date: _____

Thoughts & Impressions

_____
_____
_____
_____
_____

PRAYER

Jesus,

You know how easy it is to go back to old habits.
To hide behind strength, silence, or smiles.

But You are patient. You remind me I don't need the mask anymore.
You invite me to lean.

So today, I do just that.
I lean on You.
When I'm afraid. When I'm exposed. When I'm tempted to disappear.

I lean.

Because You are faithful, and I am still Yours.

Amen.

DAY 5

THE MIRROR AND THE MOUTH

SCRIPTURES

"As a face is reflected in water, so the heart reflects the real person."
- Proverbs 27:19 (NLT).

"Let the redeemed of the Lord say so, whom He has redeemed from trouble."
- Psalm 107:2 (ESV).

"I am the Lord your God. who brought you out of Egypt. Open your mouth wide and I will fill it."
- Psalm 81:10 (ESV).

STORY REFLECTION: YOUR WORDS SHAPE THE IMAGE YOU SEE

She stood in front of the mirror and stared like she was meeting a stranger.

Not because of the fine lines around her eyes or the tiredness in her face.

But because she didn't know who she was anymore.

Life had layered her.
Grief had shaped her posture.
Rejection had trained her to lower her eyes.
And survival had given her a script:

- Don't ask for too much.
- Don't speak too loudly.
- Don't take up too much space.

Over time, she stopped using her voice.
Not just in public, but in prayer. In her own heart.

She let silence grow roots.
Let shame take up residence.
Let other people define her reflection, and she started to believe them.

She began to echo things that were never hers to carry:

- *"I'm too complicated."*
- *"I'm not worth keeping."*
- *"I'm damaged."*
- *"I'm a debtor"*

And though no one heard it, she said it.
Every day.
Inwardly. Quietly. Consistently.

Until the day He stopped her mid-thought.

"What if you started saying what I see?"

She blinked at the mirror.
Confused. Almost offended.

Because what He saw.
It didn't match the scars she remembered.
It didn't sound like what she'd been told.
It didn't feel real.

But deep down, she wanted to believe Him.

So, she whispered it once, barely loud enough for even her own ears:

"I am loved."

And then again:

"I am chosen."

Her voice cracked. Her hands shook. But she didn't stop.

"I am seen. I am whole. I am still His."

And though her face in the mirror didn't change overnight, something in her spirit did.

She stood a little straighter.
Lifted her chin.
Looked herself in the eye, not with shame, but with growing confidence.

Because the mirror didn't hold the final say.
Her **mouth** did.

And with each word aligned with Heaven, her reflection slowly began to reveal the daughter of God she had always been.

DEVOTIONAL THOUGHT

The mirror will often lie.
But your mouth can override it.

Proverbs says the heart reflects the real person, not the wounds, not the rumors, not the regrets, but the **heart**.
And what you say to yourself has the power to shape what you see.

The enemy knows this. That's why he attacks your words.
He wants you silent.
Because silence keeps you stuck.

But Psalm 107:2 says, *"Let the redeemed of the Lord say so."*

There's power in what you say.
Power in what you stop agreeing with.
Power in what you declare, even when you don't feel it yet.

Healing deepens when your mouth begins to align with Heaven, even before the mirror catches up.

INTERACTIVE REFLECTION

1. What lies have you believed about yourself lately?
2. Where have you repeated what trauma told you instead of what God says?
3. What truths is the Spirit asking you to say *out loud* today?

QUESTION AND ANSWER

Q: What if I don't believe what I'm saying yet? Isn't that fake?

A: No, that's **faith**.

You're not pretending; you're *prophesying*.

You are speaking from a deeper place, where truth is truer than feelings, and the Word is stronger than wounds.

SCRIPTURE FOR MEDITATION:

> *"Death and life are in the power of the tongue, and those who love it will eat its fruits."*
> **- Proverbs 18:21 (ESV).**

REFLECTIVE PROMPTS:

- Write down 3 lies you've believed about yourself. Then write God's truth beside each one.
- Practice saying the truths aloud even if your voice trembles, especially if it does.

NOTES FROM MY JOURNAL

Today, I stood in front of the mirror and for the first time in a long time, I didn't rush past it.

I paused. I looked. I really *looked*.
And what I saw startled me. Not because of aging or fatigue, but because, I didn't recognize who I saw.

Not fully.

Life had slowly rewritten parts of me.
I didn't remember when I started shrinking, or when my voice got so small.
But somewhere along the way, I traded my boldness for survival.
I let pain redraw my outline and called it humility.
I let others narrate my story and called it peace.
But I felt the loss. In the silence. In the weight I carried. In the things I no longer prayed.

Then. He interrupted my spiral.
Right there, in front of the mirror.

"What if you started saying what I see?"

That question revealed something.
Could I even begin to believe that I was more than what I had absorbed from hurt, rejection, and shame?
Could I dare speak *His* truth, even if it felt foreign?

I did it anyway.
In a whisper at first. Then again, a little louder:
"I am loved. I am chosen. I am seen."

The words didn't fix everything.
But they *broke* something.
They broke the silence I'd been hiding in.

Today, I remembered that the mirror doesn't have the final word; *my mouth does.*
And every time I speak what Heaven says, I reclaim a piece of the woman I was created to be.

MY REFLECTION NOTES

(Use this space to write your thoughts, prayers, or what stood out to you today.)

_____
_____
_____
_____
_____
_____

Date: _____

Thoughts & Impressions

_____
_____
_____
_____
_____

PRAYER

Father,

I've let the mirror and the enemy tell me who I am.
I've repeated words that hurt and silenced the ones that heal.

But today, I reclaim my mouth.

Let it be an instrument of truth. Let it speak what You see, even when I don't feel it yet.

Teach me to declare healing.
To speak redemption.
To say "so" because You've redeemed me.

I am Yours.
And I will speak like it.

Amen.

DAY 6

WHEN SHE COULDN'T PRAY

SCRIPTURES

"In the same way, the Spirit helps us in our weakness. We do not know what we ought to pray for, but the Spirit himself intercedes for us through wordless groans."
- **Romans 8:26 (NIV).**

"I waited patiently for the Lord; he turned to me and heard my cry."
- **Psalm 40:1 (NIV).**

STORY REFLECTION: WHEN SILENCE SPOKE THE LOUDEST

She didn't mean to drift.
She wasn't running from God.
She just didn't know how to pray anymore.

There was no sin to confess.
No dramatic fall from grace.
Just an overwhelming silence that had taken over her soul.

She would sit down to pray, but her thoughts were scattered.
One minute she was crying, the next she was scrolling nonstop on social media.
Sometimes she just sat, numb, blank, exhausted.

She knew the right Scriptures.
She'd led the prayer meetings.
She'd been the one others came to when *they* couldn't pray.

But now?

Now she couldn't string two words together.
And the worst part? She felt like a fraud.

"How can I be someone God uses and still feel so empty?"
"How do I love a God I haven't spoken to in days?"
"What if He's disappointed in me?"

She wanted to open her mouth, but nothing would come out.
So instead, she cried.
And when the tears stopped, she just stared.
Out the window. At the ceiling. At the silence.

That's when it hit her.

Maybe this, was prayer.

Maybe prayer wasn't always poetry and power.
Maybe it was presence.
Maybe it was showing up empty and letting the Spirit speak in the gaps.

Maybe groaning counts.
Maybe sighs matter.
Maybe God listens more to tears than to words anyway.

That day, she didn't pray.
She didn't worship.
She didn't preach to her pain.

She just sat still.

And God sat with her.

And that, right there, was more than enough.

DEVOTIONAL THOUGHT

There are days when prayer feels like reaching through fog.

When words fail. When nothing flows.
When silence becomes your sanctuary and your struggle.

But Scripture says even then, you're not alone.
Romans 8:26 reminds us that the Spirit intercedes, groans, on our behalf.
Not when we're strong. Not when we're eloquent.
But when we're weak.

God doesn't need polished prayers.
He just wants you.

The tears count.
The sighs count.
The silence counts.

He hears them all.

INTERACTIVE REFLECTION

1. Have you felt guilty for not "praying enough"?
2. What would it look like to let God meet you in silence instead of performance?
3. Can you imagine God *groaning for you*, interceding when you can't?

QUESTION AND ANSWER

Q: What if I haven't prayed in a while and don't know how to start again?

A: Start with honesty.

You don't have to climb back into prayer.
Just fall into Him.

Sit with Him. Cry with Him. Let Him speak first.

He's not counting how many words you've missed.
He's counting how close He's always stayed.

SCRIPTURE FOR MEDITATION:

> *"Be still and know that I am God"*
> - **Psalm 46:10 (NIV).**

REFLECTIVE PROMPTS:

- Spend 3 minutes in complete silence with God today. Let your mind settle. Let your soul breathe.
- Write a one-line prayer, even if all it says is: *"Help."* That counts.

NOTES FROM MY JOURNAL

I didn't mean to drift.
I didn't walk away from God; I just stopped knowing how to talk to Him.
There was no rebellion in it. No bitterness.
Just exhaustion. Numbness. Silence that stretched too long.

I sat down to pray today, and nothing came out.
No eloquent words. No fire. Only tears, .raw tears coming out of brokenness.
Just me staring.
Scrolling.
Then sighing.
Then staring again.

And yet, somewhere deep in that stillness, I realized maybe this counts.
Maybe *this* is prayer too.
Maybe prayer isn't the noise.

Maybe it's the presence.
The coming. The showing up even when I feel empty.

God didn't shun me for my silence.
He didn't scold me for my stillness.
He just *sat with me*.

I didn't have to earn His attention.
I didn't have to perform to be held.
And somehow, even though I didn't "pray"…
I was heard.
I was known.
I was loved.

Maybe sighs really do count.
Maybe my silence is not distance but an invitation.

And that, today, was enough.

MY REFLECTION NOTES

(Use this space to write your thoughts, prayers, or what stood out to you today.)

_____
_____
_____
_____
_____

Date: _____

Thoughts & Impressions

_____

_____

_____

_____

_____

PRAYER

Holy Spirit,
Some days, I don't have the words.
I'm tired. I'm distracted. I feel far.

But You are near.
You groan for me when I don't know what to say.
You pray when I cannot.

Teach me to rest in Your nearness.
To trust that silence isn't distance.
And to believe that You're listening even when I'm still.

Thank You for never requiring perfection.
Just presence.

Amen.

DAY 7

WHEN THE PAST SPOKE LOUDER

SCRIPTURE:

"For I will forgive their wickedness and will remember their sins no more."
- **Hebrews 8:12 (NIV).**

STORY REFLECTION: GOODBYE, YESTERDAY

She was moving forward.
Really, she was.
New days. New chances. New declarations.
She was speaking life again, believing again and laughing again.

But the past has a sharp tongue.
And sometimes, it whispers louder than the promises.

She was having a good day when it hit her.
A simple conversation.
A smell.
A place she hadn't driven by in months.
And suddenly, the weight of who she used to be crashed down on her like a wave.

She tried to shake it off.
Tried to remind herself: That's not me anymore.

But the memories were cruel.
They didn't just remind her of what she did.
They told her what it meant:

"You'll never really be clean."

"If they knew your past, they'd walk away."
"You're pretending. God knows it. People know it. Eventually, they'll see it too."

And for a moment, she believed it.

She felt the guilt creeping up her spine.
The shame tightening around her throat.
The panic whispering: You're not healed. You're just pretending better.

She almost went silent again.
Almost shrank back.
Almost surrendered to the lie that her past disqualified her future.

But then, God interrupted the spiral.
Not with a lecture. Not with lightning.

With a memory.

A moment in prayer.
A verse she'd underlined in tears.
A whisper she'd heard months ago but never forgot:

"You are redeemed. Not recycled. Not repainted but redeemed."

And suddenly, she remembered, the past may speak loudly.
But God?
God speaks with authority.

And when He calls something new,
No voice, not even your own past, gets to overrule Him.

So, she stood up.
Not because she felt strong,
But because truth deserves to be stood on.

And even with the echoes of yesterday still in her ears,

She spoke louder:

"I am not her anymore."

And Heaven backed her up.

DEVOTIONAL THOUGHT

There are moments when the past tries to steal your future. The guilt, the shame, the fears; they can feel like an endless loop that pulls you back into who you once were. But when God declares that you are redeemed, the past has no authority over your future. You are not defined by what you've done or where you've been. You are defined by His grace, redemption, and unshakable promises.

It's easy to shrink back, to let the lies of the past dictate your worth, but God speaks a louder truth. He says: You are not your mistakes. You are not your past. You are His, and He has called you to something new. When He speaks over your life, nothing, not even your past, can stand against Him.

INTERACTIVE REFLECTION

1. Have you ever found yourself trapped by the echoes of your past?
2. What lies from your past have you allowed to define your present or future?
3. What would it look like to stand up and speak the truth of God's redemption over those lies?

QUESTION AND ANSWER

Q: How can we silence the voices of our past when they come calling?

A: We silence the voices of the past by standing on the truth of God's Word. The more we remind ourselves of what He has said about us, our identity in Christ, His forgiveness, His love, the quieter the past becomes. When we declare His truth over our lives, the power of our past loses its grip.

SCRIPTURE FOR MEDITATION:

> *"There is therefore no condemnation for those who are in Christ Jesus........."*
> - **Roman 8:1 (NIV)**.

REFLECTIVE PROMPTS

- Take a moment to listen to the voices of your past. What are they saying?
- Now, counter each lie with the truth of who you are in Christ.
- How can you declare your redemption more boldly, even in the face of past mistakes?

NOTES FROM MY JOURNAL

Today, I was moving forward, really moving.
Hope was starting to settle in again.
I felt lighter, freer, like I could finally breathe in this new chapter.
But then, the past came knocking.
Not with a bang, but with a whisper.
A scent. A phrase. A memory that snuck in without warning.
And suddenly, I felt small again.
The shame was subtle but sharp.
It didn't just remind me of what I'd done.
It tried to redefine who I am.

"You're not really healed."
"You're a fraud."
"People wouldn't love you if they knew everything."

And for a second, I almost believed it.

I almost let it pull me under again.
Almost.

But then, God spoke.
Not with thunder. Not with rebuke.
But with remembrance.

He reminded me: *I am redeemed.*
Not patched up.
Not simply improved.
Redeemed.

He reminded me that His voice outranks every whisper of the past.
That when He calls me new, no lie gets the final word.

So, I stood, shaky but sure.
Not because I feel powerful,
but because truth is worth standing on.
And today, I said it out loud, even with trembling lips:

"I am not her anymore."

And Heaven agreed.

MY REFLECTION NOTES

(Use this space to write your thoughts, prayers, or what stood out to you today.)

_____
_____
_____
_____
_____

Date: _____

Thoughts & Impressions

_____

_____

_____

_____

_____

PRAYER

Father,

Thank You for Your redemptive power. Thank You that my past does not define me, and that Your forgiveness is complete. Help me to stand firm in the truth of who I am in You, not in who I was. When the whispers of my past try to rise up, remind me of Your authority and Your promises. I declare today that I am redeemed, and my future is in Your hands in Jesus' name, Amen.

DAY 8

YOU WEREN'T LIKE THEM

SCRIPTURES

"The Lord does not look at the things people look at. People look at the outward appearance, but the Lord looks at the heart."
- **1 Samuel 16:7 (NIV).**

"You are altogether beautiful, my love; there is no flaw in you."
- **Songs of Solomon 4:7 (ESV).**

STORY REFLECTION: EMBRACING THE STRENGTH IN YOUR DIFFERENCE

You didn't belong.
At least, that's what it felt like.

You walked into the room and saw them
The composed ones.
The people who seemed to get everything right.
The ones who quoted Scriptures with ease and prayed like they had a direct line to God.

You smiled, nodded and sat down.
But inside, something in you folded.

Your story didn't sound like theirs.
They talked about breakthroughs and holiness.
You were still sorting through broken pieces.
They had highlight reels.
You had silent battles and chapters no one clapped for.

So, you stayed quiet.

You tried to blend in.
You prayed with your eyes closed, hoping no one would notice the ache behind them.

And the lie crept in softly:

> **"You can sit with them,
> but you'll never really be one of them."**

But just when shame started whispering louder.
God reminded you of something gentle, fierce, and true:

> **"You weren't made to blend in. I didn't design you
> to match. I designed you to reflect Me."**

And at that moment, your chest softened.

Maybe you didn't sound like them.
Maybe you didn't look like what "spiritual" was supposed to be.
But maybe, you were exactly who God had in mind when He shaped this moment.

Maybe you didn't come to fit in.
Maybe you came to stand out for His glory.

DEVOTIONAL THOUGHT

Comparison will starve your confidence.
And silence will shrink your soul.

You weren't called to conform; you were called to reflect.

1 Samuel 16:7 reminds us that God isn't fooled by polish or performance.
He doesn't get impressed by surface-level sameness.
He looks past the package and sees the deep place in you where authenticity lives.

You may not be like them.
But you are **l**oved, chosen, and carved by the Creator Himself.

There's no shame in standing out.
Only beauty in becoming who you truly are.

INTERACTIVE REFLECTION

1. When was the last time you felt like an outsider in a space that should have welcomed you?
2. Are there pieces of you you've hidden or changed to feel accepted?
3. What would it look like to stand fully in your story with no apology?

QUESTION AND ANSWER

Q: What if I still feel like I don't fit in, no matter how hard I try?

A: Maybe fitting in was never the point.

God didn't make you to echo others.
He made you to reflect **Him** through your voice, your path, your presence.

*The goal isn't sameness.
It's surrender.
And when you walk in the truth of who you are, you shine in ways imitation never could.

SCRIPTURE FOR MEDITATION:

"Do not conform to the pattern of this world, but be transformed by the renewing of your mind........."
  - **Romans 12:2 (NIV)**

REFLECTIVE PROMPTS:

- Write about a time you tried to shrink yourself to fit in. What did it cost you emotionally or spiritually?
- What part of you is longing to be embraced, fully and without filters?

NOTES FROM MY JOURNAL

I moved forward today.
Hope settling in.
Breathing easy in this new chapter.
But then, the past whispered.
A scent, a phrase, a memory, making me feel small again.

The shame came softly,
Telling me I wasn't truly healed.
That I was still broken.
A fraud, unworthy of love.

But God's voice cut through the noise whispering truth.
I am redeemed.
Not just fixed.
But made new.

So, I stood,
Not by my strength,
But by His truth.
"I'm not that person anymore."
And Heaven echoed back:
"Neither are you."

MY REFLECTION NOTES

(Use this space to write your thoughts, prayers, or what stood out to you today.)

_____
_____
_____
_____

Date: _____

Thoughts & Impressions

_____
_____
_____
_____

PRAYER

Father,

I've spent too long trying to match a mold You never made. Trying to talk like them, dress like them and pray like them.

But You see me.
You know me.
You call me good, even in my difference.

Help me embrace the version of me You had in mind all along.
Let me walk in authenticity, not performance.
Let me reflect You, not blend into them.

In Jesus' name,
Amen.

DAY 9

THE FEAR OF BEING TOO MUCH

SCRIPTURES

"My dove, in the clefts of the rock, in the hiding places on the mountainside, show me your face, let me hear your voice: for your voice is sweet, and your ace is lovely."
- **Songs of Solomon 2:14. (NIV).**

"Turn your eyes away from me, for they overwhelm me."
- **Songs of Solomon 6:5. (NIV).**

"For the Lord takes pleasure in His people; He adorns the humble with salvation."
- **Psalm 149:4. (ESV).**

STORY REFLECTION: WHEN SHE FELT LIKE TOO MUCH AND NOT ENOUGH

She had only just begun to settle into her skin.
A new rhythm of breathing without apology.
A brave quietness had begun to rise in her chest, the kind that comes when shame begins to loosen its grip.

But then...................
The reactions came.

She opened her heart.
Spoke her truth without polish.
Cried harder than she meant to in a room that wasn't ready.
She laughed deeply, and someone flinched.

Not everyone.

But just enough to make her doubt again.
To make her shrink again.

Their silence screamed louder than words.
Their smiles dimmed just slightly.
She knew that look. The unspoken:
"You're too much."
"Too emotional. Too messy. Too real."

It pulled her backward, like wind against a fragile door.
She had been here before.
Where vulnerability felt like a sin, and presence too loud for the room.

And in her spirit, she wanted to run.
To hide.
To perform again.

She stood before the mirror, remembering the masks—the curated quiet.

The practiced laugh.

The way she had learned to disappear just enough to be loved.

Then a whisper.

"Turn your eyes away from Me, for they overwhelm Me."

The words fell like warm oil down her bruised soul.

Could it be?
That her rawness didn't repulse Him, it ravished Him?
Her honesty didn't scare Him, it moved Him?
Her messy heart didn't disappoint Him, it delighted Him?

He saw her, not just tolerated, but treasured.

In the book where lovers whisper their longings, He had written hers too.
In that gaze, she wasn't too much.
She wasn't even "just enough."
She was more than enough.
Altogether lovely. Flawless in His eyes, not because she had no pain, but because He loved every scar she dared to reveal.

He didn't step back.
He stepped closer.

DEVOTIONAL THOUGHT

In a world that teaches women to shrink in order to be loved, it is radical to stand as you are, unfiltered, unpolished, and unapologetic.

But the Lover of your soul never asked you to shrink.

His love doesn't blink at your intensity.

It welcomes it.

Your tears, your laughter, your truth; they are music to His ears.

He is not overwhelmed.

He is captivated.

INTERACTIVE REFLECTION

1. What have you been told is "too much" about you?
2. How do you edit yourself to feel safer or more acceptable to others?
3. When was the last time you felt truly seen and accepted?

QUESTION AND ANSWER

Q: What if people pull away when I show who I really am?

A: Some will. But the One who matters most never turns away. He draws near. And the people He sends to your life won't need you to shrink; they'll love you in your fullness.

SCRIPTURES FOR MEDITATION

- *"I praise you because I am fearfully and wonderfully made………."* - **Psalm 139:14. (NIV).**
- *"Though the mountains be shaken, my unfailing love for you will not be shaken………"* - **Isaiah 54:10. (NIV).**

REFLECTIVE PROMPTS

- Journal a moment you felt like "too much" for someone. How did that shape you?
- Ask God to help you unlearn the lie that your fullness is a flaw.
- Write down the parts of yourself you've been hiding and invite Jesus into those spaces.

NOTES FROM MY JOURNAL

I had just begun to breathe without apology.
Until their reactions made me want to shrink again.

The old fear whispered: *"You're too much."*

But then I heard Him:

> *"Turn your eyes away from Me, for they overwhelm Me."*
> - **Songs of Solomon 6:5. (ESV).**

Not too much. Not barely enough.

Altogether lovely.

He didn't step back.
He stepped closer.

MY REFLECTION NOTES

(Use this space to write your thoughts, prayers, or what stood out to you today.)

_____
_____
_____
_____
_____

Date: _____

Thoughts & Impressions

_____
_____
_____
_____
_____

PRAYER

Jesus,

Thank You for loving the whole of me. Not just the quiet parts. Not just the strong parts.

But the loud, tearful, and honest places too.

You are not scared off by my depth, You made me this way.

Help me live in the freedom of being fully seen and loved.

Teach me not to shrink. Teach me to stand.

In Your eyes, I am not too much.

I am Yours.

Amen.

DAY 10

DARK AND LOVELY: RECLAIMING MY VINEYARD

SCRIPTURE

"Dark am I, yet lovely, O daughters of Jerusalem, dark like the tents of Kedar, like the tent curtains of Solomon. Do not stare at me because I am dark, because I am darkened by the sun. My mother's sons were angry with me and made me take care of the vineyards; my own vineyard I had to neglect."
- **Songs of Solomon 1:5–6 (NIV)**

STORY REFLECTION: THE VINEYARD WAS HERS

She looked at her hands, calloused, tired, beautifully worn.

They had built things. Held things together. Wiped tears. Carried burdens. Sown into vineyards that were never hers. She had held everyone else's dreams, healed other people's pain, fought for families, friends, and futures that didn't include her.

But now, for the first time in a long time, she sat still. And when the silence didn't crush her, she realized something:

She had a vineyard, too.

Her own.

She had neglected it for years, told herself there wasn't time. That one day, maybe, when the kids were grown, when the debt was paid off, when things settled… then she would return to it.

But the sun had already scorched her skin. The wind had already shaped her frame. The labor had already left its marks. And in the mirror, she saw it clearly:

She was dark, but she was lovely.

Not lovely in spite of the scars. Lovely because of them.

The sun-darkened skin wasn't shame; it was proof she showed up. That she endured. That she gave. That she survived.

She remembered the verse she'd once underlined in a season of private ache:

"Dark am I, yet lovely."

And now it sang over her. A banner of beauty. Of worth. Of return.

She whispered to herself, as if awakening a forgotten truth:

"I have a vineyard. And it's worth tending."

She no longer felt selfish for choosing rest. For watering her soul. For breathing deep and dreaming again.

It wasn't vanity. It was stewardship. It was worship. It was healing.

The world taught her that her value came from labor, that if she wasn't doing, she wasn't worthy. But God never measured her by output, only by love.

And so, with trembling hands and steady heart, she picked up her tools, not for someone else's garden, but her own.

It was time to come home to herself.

DEVOTIONAL THOUGHT

There comes a sacred turning point when you realize that your soul has a vineyard and God is calling you back to it.

Not out of guilt, but out of grace. Not because you failed others, but because He never forgot you.

Song of Songs 1:5 - 6 is a whispered anthem for every woman who has been stretched, sunburnt, and silenced by responsibility. Who has tended everyone else's ground while her own withered.

But now, now, the season shifts. This is your invitation to stop apologizing for needing care. To stop hiding your scars. To reclaim your vineyard.

You are dark, but you are lovely.

You are weathered, but you are worthy.

And your vineyard? It's still yours.

INTERACTIVE REFLECTION

1. Whose vineyard have you been tending at the cost of your own?
2. What lies have you believed about your worth being tied to performance?
3. What would it look like to begin reclaiming your inner life, your vineyard today?

QUESTION AND ANSWER

Q: Is it selfish to take time for myself after giving so much to others?

A: No. It is sacred. Even Jesus withdrew to be alone with the Father. Reclaiming your vineyard isn't neglecting others, it's letting God restore you so you can flourish from a place of fullness, not depletion.

SCRIPTURE FOR MEDITATION

"There I will give her back her vineyards, and will make the Valley of Achor [a] a door of hope. There she will respond [b] as in the days of her youth, as in the day she came up out of Egypt"
- **Hosea 2:15 (AMP)**

REFLECTIVE PROMPTS

- Write down the areas of your life you've neglected.
- Ask God to show you how to tend to your own soul again.
- What would "watering your vineyard" look like this week, spiritually, emotionally, or physically?

NOTES FROM MY JOURNAL

I've poured out so much for others that I forgot what it felt like to pour into me.

I used to think rest was a reward. Now, I know it's a rhythm.

I used to feel guilty for slowing down. Now, I see the beauty in being still.

Today, I remembered God never asked me to disappear for others to thrive. He invites me to rise, too.

My vineyard is not beyond repair.

It's mine.

And it's time.

MY REFLECTION NOTES

(Use this space to write your thoughts, prayers, or what stood out to you today.)

_____
_____
_____
_____
_____

Date: _____

Thoughts & Impressions

_____
_____
_____
_____
_____
_____
_____

PRAYER

Father,

Thank You for seeing me, sun-scorched, weary, yet still lovely.

Thank You for reminding me that I have not been forgotten.

Teach me to come home to myself, to tend the places in me that have been left dry for too long.

I surrender the guilt. I release the shame.

And I receive this invitation to return, rebuild, and rest.

This is my vineyard. And I will nurture it because You say it's worth it.

DAY 11

WHEN SHE LOOKED BACK AND SAW

SCRIPTURES

"Who is this coming up from the wilderness leaning on her beloved?"
- **Songs of Solomon 8:5a. (NKJV).**

"You hem me in, behind and before, and you lay your hand upon me."
- **Psalm 139:5. (NIV).**

STORY REFLECTION: WHEN SHE LOOKED BACK AND SAW

The wind shifted that morning.
There was no thunder, no flash of divine light.
Just stillness.
A sacred hush in the air.
And something inside her, maybe the Spirit, maybe a memory, whispered, *"Turn around."*

She hesitated.

She had walked so far, through tears that tasted like salt and iron, through nights that stretched like unending tunnels. Her sandals were worn thin, her heart even thinner. And though her steps had become steadier, her soul still flinched at the thought of what she'd left behind.

But the voice came again, clearer this time.
"Look back, not to return, but to remember."

She inhaled deeply.

Turned slowly.
And for the first time in a long time, she didn't avert her eyes from the past.

What she saw caught her breath.
Not ruins.
Not shame.
Not a girl too broken to stand.

She saw a path, wounded, yes, but sacred.
Footsteps in the mud, where she had once collapsed.
Tears watered into the earth like prayers.
Moments where grief had buckled her knees; and somehow, those were the places blooming now.

She saw Him.

He had been there, through the groaning nights, the whispered "whys," the desperate prayers when rent was due. When her friends used and betrayed her, plunging her into an unending road of debt. When the phone lit up with another message from a creditor demanding what she no longer had, she.
had walked that road with guilt hanging off her like a second skin.
With whispers behind her back and pity in front of her face.
With fingers pointing and mouths muttering, "She brought this on herself."

But He never pointed.
Never whispered.
He just stayed. Silent sometimes, but steady.

He lifted her when shame clawed at her throat.
He carried her when her body moved, but her spirit couldn't.
And now, standing here, looking back, she realized………..

She wasn't just a survivor.

She was a witness.

Of grace.
Of glory.
Of a God who didn't wait on the other side of the storm, but who walked through it with her.

She smiled, a real one. Not the polite one she had worn for years. This smile was born of battle and mercy and something unshakable. She turned back around, faced the horizon, and whispered with conviction:
"I'm not who I was, but He has always been who He is."

She didn't just walk out of the wilderness.
She rose from it.

Leaning on her Beloved.
Glowing with quiet strength.
Proof that ashes can still birth beauty, and scars can still sing.

DEVOTIONAL THOUGHT

We often fear looking back because we're afraid the old pain will swallow us again. But sometimes, God invites us to remember, not to relive the pain, but to recognize the Presence that carried us.

It's not about glorifying the wilderness. It's about testifying of the God who brought us through it.

Looking back can be holy, when we see not just the scars, but the steady hand of grace that kept us breathing, hoping, healing.

INTERACTIVE REFLECTION

1. Do you find it hard to look back at certain seasons in your life? Why?

2. What would happen if you looked for evidence of God's presence instead of just the pain?
3. Can you identify a moment where you now realize God was carrying you?

QUESTION AND ANSWER

Q: What if my past still feels too heavy to face?

A: Then don't face it alone. Lean into the One who walked you through it. Ask Him to show you where He was in those moments. Healing begins when we see not just what we went through, but Who brought us through.

SCRIPTURE FOR MEDITATION

"Who is this coming up from the wilderness, leaning upon her beloved?"
- Songs of Solomon 8:5a (NKJV)

REFLECTIVE PROMPTS

- Journal about a wilderness season you thought you'd never survive.
- Write a letter to your younger self during that time, from the perspective of grace.
- Sit quietly and ask God to highlight where He was in those moments.

NOTES FROM MY JOURNAL

I looked back, not to grieve but to remember.

I didn't see failure.

I saw footsteps.

I saw where He met me, carried me, wept with me.

The shame that once wrapped around me now looks like soil where grace grew roots.

I am not who I was.
But He has always been who He is.

And that is my testimony.

MY REFLECTION NOTES

(Use this space to write your thoughts, prayers, or what stood out to you today.)

_____
_____
_____
_____
_____

Date: _____

Thoughts & Impressions

_____
_____
_____
_____
_____

PRAYER

Father,

Thank You for walking with me through every hard place. When I look back now, help me not to see shame, but Your shadow beside me. Let me remember Your mercy, not my mistakes. Teach me to wear my past as a testimony, not a chain. And may I always lean on You, not just in brokenness, but in healing. Amen.

DAY 12

THE PURPOSE WITHIN THE PAIN

SCRIPTURES

"For I know the plans I have for you," declares the Lord, "plans to prosper you and not to harm you, plans to give you a hope and a future."
- **Jeremiah 29:11 (NIV)**

"We are hard pressed on every side, but not crushed; perplexed, but not in despair; persecuted, but not abandoned; struck down, but not destroyed."
- **2 Corinthians 4:8-9 (NIV)**

STORY REFLECTION: THE HIDDEN GIFTS

It's funny, she thought, how pain can trick you into believing that the struggle is the end.

That the brokenness is where it stops.

There were days when she felt like she was drowning. The weight of expectations. The long nights, the empty prayers, the endless questions. Why did this happen? How could this be happening? She had no answers, only the ache of it all.

And yet, today, something was different.
Her heart, which had once felt like shattered glass, had begun to beat with a quiet kind of strength.

She could almost feel the invisible thread that had been woven through every part of her journey, the victories, failures, moments when she wanted to give up, and the moments when she wanted to hide. All of them had led her here, to this place of understanding.

She sat still for a moment, in the warmth of that realization. The pain was not without reason. The hurt, the loss, the things that had left her feeling empty it all had meaning now. Because, somewhere in the middle of it all, there had been a whisper: *This isn't for nothing.*

And it wasn't.

The scars on her heart weren't just remnants of wounds. They were proof that she had survived, not on her own, but with the strength of something greater than herself. The lies she once believed had been dismantled. The fears had lost their power. The darkness, though it still lingered, no longer felt like it would consume her. She was no longer behind the mask.

In the midst of it, there was hope. There was a purpose. There was a future.

It was as if she could see it all clearly now. Her pain had shaped her. It had been the kiln, the fire, that had refined the gold she had become. What she once saw as defeat, she now saw as a stepping stone to a deeper understanding of God's love.

She realized that she was never meant to stay broken. She wasn't meant to be trapped in the cycle of pain without progress. The scars weren't signs of her defeat; they were markers of her journey, and they told the story of a woman who had risen.

Her pain had been the catalyst.

It had been the fire that forged the woman who could stand here, healed and whole, with a story to tell.

It wasn't just about her anymore. She wasn't the only one who needed to hear her story. Others did too. And that realization settled in her chest, warm and real:

Her pain had purpose. It had brought her here. It had made her a vessel for healing.

Her heart wasn't just broken; it was *remade*.

DEVOTIONAL THOUGHT

In the most difficult moments of your journey, God is at work. He doesn't waste a single moment of your suffering. In fact, He turns the ashes into something beautiful, and the pain into something powerful. Every tear, every heartbreak, every moment of doubt is all woven into the larger tapestry of His plan for your life.

What you may see as defeat, He sees as the making of a masterpiece. Your story of pain is not over; it's just the beginning of a story of hope, restoration, and purpose.

INTERACTIVE REFLECTION

1. Reflect on a painful moment in your life. How did it shape you? What good has come from it, even if it's hard to see right now?
2. In what ways do you believe God can use your struggles to impact others?
3. How can you start seeing your pain as a part of your purpose today?

QUESTION AND ANSWER

Q: How can my pain have any purpose, Father? It feels like it was just for nothing.

God: I don't waste pain. Every part of your journey has led you to this place. I am using all of it, the heartache, the loss, the waiting, to build something beautiful in you and through you. You are not forgotten. You are being made into someone who will shine with my glory. Trust that your pain is part of a greater purpose.

NOTES FROM MY JOURNAL

I used to think pain was the end of the story.
But today, I see it differently.

The ache shaped me.
The scars speak now.
Not of what broke me,
but of how He rebuilt me.

My pain had purpose.
And now, so do I.

MY REFLECTION NOTES

(Use this space to write your thoughts, prayers, or what stood out to you today.)

_____
_____
_____
_____
_____

Date: _____

Thoughts & Impressions

_____

_____

_____

_____

_____

> **PRAYER**
>
> Father,
>
> I bring my pain before You today, knowing that You are the One who redeems it. You take what the enemy meant for harm and use it for Your glory. I trust that my suffering is not in vain, and that You are making something beautiful from ashes. Help me to see the purpose in my pain. Open my eyes to how You've used the struggles to build my character, my faith, and my hope. Let me walk boldly in the knowledge that every part of my story matters and it's all being woven together to reveal Your masterpiece.
>
> **Amen.**

DAY 13

THE STRENGTH TO KEEP SHOWING UP

SCRIPTURES

"You intended to harm me, but God intended it for good to accomplish what is now being done, the saving of many lives."
- Genesis 50:20. (NIV)

"He comforts us in all our troubles so that we can comfort others."
- 2 Corinthians 1:4a (NLT)

STORY REFLECTION: HE GAVE ME BEAUTY FOR ASHES

She had only meant to show up, not to be seen.

Still a little tender from her journey, she quietly slid into the back row of that gathering.

No spotlight. No grand entrance.

Just one foot in front of the other, showing up, one breath at a time.

She didn't expect to speak.
She didn't expect her voice not to shake.
And she certainly didn't expect what happened next.

It started with a question.
A woman near her stammered softly, "How…did you………. get through?"

She hesitated. That old fear flickered

"What if they judge me? What if it's too much?"

THE MASK SHE WORE: THE REBIRTH MADELINE AGOBA

But something in her had shifted. The silence no longer fit her.

So, she shared.
Not everything.
Just enough.
Just the truth.

About the mask.
The weight.
The shame.
The collapse.
The Voice that stayed when everyone else left.
The rebuilding, the quiet days when healing felt too slow to be holy.

She was mid-sentence when she noticed it.
Another woman's eyes were brimming with tears.
Another was nodding.
One reached out and gently squeezed her hand.

That's when she knew: her pain had not been pointless.

Every long night.
Every whispered prayer through gritted teeth.
Every shame-drenched memory that He had lovingly untangled.
It was all rising now, not as a flood to drown her, but a fountain to refresh others.

She realized she wasn't just surviving anymore.
She was *planting*.

She had become the place someone else found safety.
She, once the girl who thought she had nothing to offer, was now a lighthouse for hearts drifting in the dark.

And it wasn't because she was perfect.
It was because she was present.

In that moment, the ache of her past met the hand of the Father and gave birth to *purpose*.

She didn't need to pretend.
She didn't need to perform.
She just needed to be *available*.
Because when He healed her, He didn't just set her free;
He sent her.

DEVOTIONAL THOUGHT

Pain doesn't always end in the graveyard. Sometimes, it ends in a garden.

God never wastes your tears. He bottles them.
He doesn't just wipe your wounds clean; He uses them.
To draw others.
To heal others.
To free others.

This is the beautiful mystery of grace: Your wounds can become someone else's welcome mat.

Don't underestimate the power of what you've survived.
There is someone praying tonight for a voice like yours to show them the way home.

INTERACTIVE REFLECTION

1. Can you recall a time when your vulnerability helped someone feel safe?
2. What parts of your story still feel "too messy" to be used? Ask God about those.
3. Who in your life may need your voice, your presence, your story right now?

QUESTION AND ANSWER

Q: "Why did I have to go through all that?"

God: "So that others would know there's a way through. And so they'd see Me in you."

SCRIPTURE FOR MEDITATION

"As an apple tree among the trees of the forest, so is my beloved among the young men. With great delight i sat in his shadow, and his fruit was sweet to my taste. He brought me to the banqueting house and his banner over me was love." - **Songs of Solomon 2:3-4. (NKJV).**

REFLECTIVE PROMPTS

- List one area of your life where your pain now helps someone else.
- Reflect on what "purpose through pain" looks like for you right now.
- Ask: "God, how can I use my healing to help another today?"

NOTES FROM MY JOURNAL

I thought I was just surviving.
But then I opened my mouth, and someone else exhaled.

My pain wasn't pointless.
It planted something.
And when I spoke, healing echoed.

I don't need to be perfect.
I just need to be present.
He didn't just free me; He sent me

MY REFLECTION NOTES

(Use this space to write your thoughts, prayers, or what stood out to you today.)

_____
_____
_____
_____
_____
_____

Date: _____

Thoughts & Impressions

_____
_____
_____
_____
_____
_____
_____

PRAYER

Dear Father,

You are the God who turns graves into gardens.

You held me through the pain, and now You invite me to help others find You there too.

Thank You for not wasting a single tear.

Thank You for trusting me with testimony.

I no longer see my story as a mistake, but as a miracle in motion.

Use me. Use the cracks, the scars, the healed places, and even the ones still healing.

May my life whisper hope to the hurting

And may my past now point the way to freedom.

In Jesus' name,

Amen.

DAY 14

WHEN THE SILENCE SPEAKS

SCRIPTURES

"I am my beloved's, and his desire is for me."
- **Songs of Solomon 7:10. (NKJV)**

"In quietness and confidence shall be your strength."
- **Isaiah 30:15. (NKJV)**

"Your ears shall hear a word behind you, saying, 'This is the way, walk in it,' when you turn to the right or when you turn to the left."
- **Isaiah 30:21. (NKJV)**

STORY REFLECTION: WHEN WORDS FAIL, THE HEART FINDS ITS VOICE

For so long, she believed strength meant always being loud, always pushing, always moving, always busy.
If she slowed down, wouldn't everything fall apart?
If she grew quiet, wouldn't she disappear?

But now, she wasn't afraid of silence anymore.

At first, it felt like emptiness, a space too vast, too vulnerable.
But slowly, the hush began to breathe.
It wrapped around her like a soft cloak, not suffocating, but sacred.
Not heavy with judgment, but light with presence.

It wasn't silence that hurt her before.
It was what the world shouted into it: condemnation, comparison, shame.
But now………….. the noise had faded.

And in the stillness, she began to hear something truer.

A whisper not from her wounds, but from the One who stayed.
A knowing that didn't demand performance.
A steady voice saying, *"You're not forgotten."*
"You're not too late."
"You're not too much."

There was no rush here.
No pressure to get it all right.
Just breath. Just healing. Just quiet restoration.

And in that quiet, she began to rise.

She didn't need the spotlight to prove she mattered.
She didn't need the applause to confirm her place.
She was steady, because she was rooted.
She was at peace, because she was held.

She had tried noise. She had tried effort. She had tried pretending.
But now, she was trying stillness.
And in that stillness, she was finally becoming whole.

Because the strength she needed wasn't in striving.
It was in surrender.

In quietness and in confidence, she found her strength.
Not the kind that fights to be seen,
But the kind that stands still................ and is.

DEVOTIONAL THOUGHT

God's silence is not His absence.
Sometimes, it's His most tender language.

In the silence, He is not testing you.
He is grounding you.

Rooting you.
Realigning your soul with the truth that can't be shaken.

When the noise clears, you start to hear things that were always true, you just weren't still enough to receive them.

This is the part of your story where your *dignity* returns.
Not borrowed. Not begged for. Not given by people who could take it back.
But dignity birthed in the hush of God's presence.

INTERACTIVE REFLECTION

1. When you sit in silence with God, what emotions surface first? Why?
2. What part of you feels like it's slowly waking up again?
3. What would it look like to stop performing and just *be*?

QUESTION AND ANSWER

Q: *What if I've spent so long hiding that I don't know who I am anymore?*

A: The silence is where God gently peels back every false identity. You don't need to rush it. Who you are is not lost; she's just been waiting to be welcomed back.

SCRIPTURE FOR MEDITATION

- *"For thus said the Lord God, the Holy One of Israel, in returning and rest you shall be saved. In quietness and confidence shall be your strength."* - **Isaiah 30:15. (NKJV).**

REFLECTIVE PROMPTS

- Write a list titled *"Who I Thought I Had to Be"*. Then, beside it, write *"Who God Says I Am."*

- Spend 5 minutes in silence. No music. No noise. Just breath and being.

    Journal what you feel afterward.

NOTES FROM MY JOURNAL

I used to fear silence.
I thought if I stopped moving, I'd disappear.
But in the quiet, I found something stronger than noise:
I found Presence.
And it didn't demand anything from me.
It simply stayed.

Here without performing, pushing, or pretending,
I'm becoming whole.

MY REFLECTION NOTES

(Use this space to write your thoughts, prayers, or what stood out to you today.)

_____
_____
_____
_____
_____

Date: _____

Thoughts & Impressions

_____
_____
_____
_____
_____

PRAYER

Lord, I thank You for the quiet places,
not because they're easy,
but because they're holy.

In this silence, teach me to hear again.
Let me find my name in Your voice, not their opinions.
Let me shed the shame and stand in love.
And when I start to remember who I am…………..
Help me believe her.

Amen.

DAY 15

THE QUIET STRENGTH

SCRIPTURES

"I have calmed and quieted my soul, like a weaned child with its mother; like a weaned child is my soul within me."
- Psalm 131:2 (AMP)

"The quiet words of the wise are more than to be heeded than the shouts of a ruler of fools."
- Ecclesiastes 9:17 (MSB)

STORY REFLECTION: WHEN SILENCE HOLDS POWER, STRENGTH IS QUIETLY FORGED

She had come to understand that there was a sacred kind of strength in silence. Strength that wasn't about forcing her way through the noise of life or trying to prove herself. The world had always been loud, demanding, rushing, pushing. But in the quiet, she discovered a peace she hadn't known existed.

For so long, she had believed that to be strong. She needed to keep moving, to keep fighting, to keep proving that she was enough. But now, in the stillness, she felt a different kind of strength, one that didn't need to be seen or applauded. It was a strength that came from trusting that God was already at work, even in the silence.

In the quietness, she didn't have to perform or strive. She didn't have to put on a face or wear a mask. She didn't have to fill the space with words or action. She simply had to be. And in that stillness, she found herself rooted anchored, not in what she did, but in who she was in Him.

The world had tried to push her into molds, to make her conform to standards that were never hers. But in this sacred quiet, she realized that her strength wasn't in her accomplishments or her ability to keep up with the noise. Her strength was in resting in His presence, in surrendering to His timing, in trusting that He was enough.

For the first time in a long while, she wasn't afraid of the silence. She welcomed it, knowing that in it, God was shaping her. And as she sat in the quiet, she heard His voice, soft, steady, and unwavering. "You are enough. You are loved. I am here."

The quietness was no longer a place of fear. It was the very place where her strength grew, rooted in His love and grace.

DEVOTIONAL THOUGHT

In a world that values productivity and noise, it can be hard to embrace stillness. But it is in quietness and trust that we find our true strength. This isn't a passive strength; it's a quiet confidence that comes from knowing that God is working in us, even when we can't see it. When we stop striving, we make room for His power to transform us from the inside out.

INTERACTIVE REFLECTION

1. How do you feel when you are still and silent? Does it bring peace or discomfort?
2. What might it look like for you to embrace quietness today, even if only for a few moments?
3. How can you trust God more in times of quietness, instead of feeling the need to fill the space with activity?

QUESTION AND ANSWER

Q: How do I know that God is still working when I am quiet?

A: God works in quietness just as powerfully as He does in the noise. Sometimes, the most profound transformations happen in the moments of stillness when we're simply resting in His presence. Trust that in these quiet moments, God is healing, restoring, and preparing you for what's ahead.

SCRIPTURE FOR MEDITATION

"You will keep in perfect peace those whose minds are steadfast, because they trust in You."
- Isaiah 26:3 (NIV)

REFLECTIVE PROMPT

- Take a moment today to be still and listen. What do you hear in the silence?
- How can you create space for quietness in your routine, allowing God to move in you?

NOTES FROM MY JOURNAL

The world told me I had to be loud to be heard.
But I've learned to be still and still stand.

In the quiet, I found strength that didn't beg to be seen.
Not the kind that roars.
But the kind that roots.
That breathes.
That stays.

And in that stillness, I heard Him whisper:
"You are already enough."

MY REFLECTION NOTES

(Use this space to write your thoughts, prayers, or what stood out to you today.)

_____
_____
_____
_____
_____
_____

Date: _____

Thoughts & Impressions

_____
_____
_____
_____
_____

PRAYER

Father,

Thank You for the quiet strength that You offer. Help me to embrace stillness and trust in Your presence. In a world that demands noise and constant motion, teach me to rest in You. Let me find peace in the silence, knowing that You are working in ways I cannot see. I surrender my need to perform and trust that You are enough. May Your quiet strength be my foundation in Jesus' name,

Amen.

DAY 16

THE UNSEEN WORK OF GROWTH

SCRIPTURE

> "The fig tree forms its early fruit; the blossoming vines spread their fragrance. Arise, come, my darling; my beautiful one, come with me."
> - **Songs of Solomon 2:13 (NIV)**

> "For the earth brings forth its crops by itself; first the blade, then the ear, then the full grain in the ear."
> - **Mark 4:28 (ESV)**

> "Being confident of this, that he who began a good work in you will carry it onto completion until the day of Christ Jesus."
> - **Philippians 1:6 (NIV)**

STORY REFLECTION: "THE BEAUTY IN THE WAITING"

She had always been in a hurry. First, a hurry not to be seen and then a hurry to be seen. A hurry to be known. A hurry to prove that she was capable, valuable, and ready for everything life had to offer. She had spent so many years chasing the end result, thinking that success meant a finished product, a completed journey, and public validation.

But today, as she stood quietly in the corner of her room, reflecting on how far she had come, something inside her shifted. For the first time, she realized that the beauty of her transformation wasn't in the grand moments, the accolades, or the applause; it was in the small, unseen acts that no one noticed. It was the moments when she chose to keep going, even when no one was watching.

She thought about the seasons when she was hidden away, when she couldn't see the progress or measure the growth. The times when it felt like nothing was happening, but all the while, God was working behind the scenes. It was like the plant that grew deep roots before it ever reached the surface. The blade of grass didn't show itself until the right time. The fruit didn't appear overnight; it took months, maybe even years, to ripen.

And as she reflected on the quiet years, the times when it seemed like nothing was moving, when all she could see was the soil and darkness, she began to understand. The growth that had happened in her heart, in her spirit, in her mind, was a slow and sacred process.

What had seemed like a dormant season now felt like the tender years of preparation. She began to see the beauty in the patience it took to allow the soil of her soul to be softened by God. It was in that quiet, unseen work that she found strength she never knew she had. The patience. The waiting. The nurturing.

She realized that God was never in a hurry. He didn't need her to rush into anything. He wasn't looking for the fruit of her labor to appear all at once. He simply needed her to trust the process.

There was no pressure to perform. No deadline to meet. She could rest in the fact that, just as the earth brings forth crops in its time, so too was her life unfolding in its own season.

In the moments when she felt like nothing was happening, God was working. In the times when she felt invisible, He was strengthening her roots, preparing her for what was ahead.

It wasn't the big leaps that made the difference; it was the small, steady steps of faith. She didn't have to rush to the finish line. God was faithful to finish what He had started, and He was working even when she didn't feel it. Her role was to trust the process and embrace the quiet moments.

DEVOTIONAL THOUGHT

It's easy to look at the journey of life and feel disheartened when we're in a waiting season, when we don't see the growth we expect or desire. But it's in the quiet, unseen moments that God is doing some of His most profound work. He is cultivating patience in us, deepening our trust in His timing, and strengthening our roots for the future.

We can often feel like we're not moving fast enough or like others are ahead of us in their journey. But just as the earth brings forth its crops slowly and steadily, God is working in us, and His timing is always perfect. When we learn to trust His process and embrace the waiting, we find peace in knowing that He is doing something valuable in us, even if it's not visible to others.

Remember, the work God is doing in you is never wasted. Every moment of waiting, every season of silence, is an opportunity for growth. Trust that He who began a good work in you will continue it, and He will be faithful to bring it to completion at the right time.

INTERACTIVE REFLECTION

1. Have you ever felt frustrated by the pace of your growth?
2. Have you compared yourself to others and wondered why your journey felt slower? Reflect on a season of waiting in your life.
3. What did you learn during that time that you couldn't have learned in a season of immediate success?
4. How did God shape you during that period of silence?

QUESTION AND ANSWER

Q: What parts of your life are you trying to rush or push forward? How can you trust God's timing and allow Him to unfold His plans for you at the pace that He knows is best?

A: Growth is not a race; it is a sacred unfolding. So, breathe, surrender, and let your roots grow deeper-even if it means waiting quietly while the fruit remains unseen.

SCRIPTURE FOR MEDITATION

"Wait for the Lord; be strong, and let your heart take courage; wait for the Lord."
- **Psalm 27:14 (NIV)**

"Let your roots grow down into him, and let your lives be built on him."
- **Colossians 2:7 (NLT)**

REFLECTIVE PROMPT

Think about the areas in your life where you are currently waiting for breakthrough, growth, or direction. How can you embrace the process and trust that God is working in you during this season? What areas do you need to let go of control and simply trust in God's perfect timing?

NOTES FROM MY JOURNAL

I used to rush, thinking speed meant strength, and being seen meant I mattered.

But God was never in a hurry.
He worked in silence.

Deep beneath the surface.

What felt like stillness was sacred becoming.
What seemed like delay was quiet preparation.

Now I know
The hidden years held me.
The waiting shaped me.
And even when I saw nothing,
He was growing everything.

MY REFLECTION NOTES

(Use this space to write your thoughts, prayers, or what stood out to you today.)

_____
_____
_____
_____
_____

Date: _____

Thoughts & Impressions

_____
_____
_____
_____
_____

PRAYER

Lord, thank You for the work You are doing in me, even when I can't see it. Help me to embrace the seasons of waiting and growth, trusting that You are preparing me for something beautiful. Strengthen my heart, and help me to have patience, knowing that You are in control. I surrender my need to rush the process and trust that You will bring the fruit of my labor in Your perfect time.

Amen.

DAY 17

BECOMING RADIANT

SCRIPTURE

"Who is this that appears like the dawn, fair as the moon, bright as the sun, majestic as the stars in procession?"
- **Songs of Solomon 6:10 (NIV)**

STORY REFLECTION: "WHEN SHE LOOKED AGAIN: THE MORNING SHE MET HERSELF"

There was a morning unlike the others.

The sun peeked in gently through the old lace curtain, throwing golden lines across the room like heaven's own highlighter. She was getting ready, same routine, same mirror, same face. Yet, this time, she paused.
Not because she had nowhere to go or something to fix.
But because something inside her whispered, "Look again."

She tilted her head, brushed the loose strands from her face, and looked. Not at the worn-out eyes or the faint wrinkles that told stories no one had time to ask about.
But at the woman inside.

And for the first time in a long time, she didn't sigh.

She didn't scold herself or pick herself apart.
She didn't try to put on strength like makeup or stuff down her fears like foundation.
She didn't whisper, "You're such a mess."
Instead, she whispered, "You're still here."
And it wrecked her in the most beautiful way.

THE MASK SHE WORE: THE REBIRTH MADELINE AGOBA

She remembered the days she didn't want to rise.
The nights she cried herself to sleep.
The burdens that had no name but sat heavy on her chest.
The debt.
The gossip.
The shame.
The pretending.

She remembered when her voice trembled in every room because she was so afraid of taking up space.
She remembered the ones who looked past her, through her, and sometimes through with her.
She remembered how she used to disappear in plain sight.

But now, she wasn't invisible anymore.

No, she hadn't won the lottery. She hadn't been rescued by a prince or had all the pieces magically fall into place.

But she had survived.
She had fought.
She had dared to show up, day after day, when quitting would have been easier.
She had found beauty in the breaking and strength in the silence.
She had learned that not all glow-ups come with glitter; some come with grit.

And standing there, in the same old mirror she used to avoid, she saw a different woman.

Her shoulders didn't carry shame anymore; they carried stories.
Her eyes no longer darted around in fear; they steadied, warm and wise.
Her mouth no longer stayed silent to stay safe; it had begun to speak life.

This wasn't arrogance. It wasn't vanity.
It was resurrection.

She was rising, not like a storm, but like the dawn.
Soft. Quiet. Unstoppable.

And she finally understood.
Radiance wasn't about being flawless. It was about being found.
Found in grace.
Found in purpose.
Found in God.

DEVOTIONAL THOUGHT

Becoming radiant doesn't always feel like a grand transformation.
Sometimes, it's subtle, slow, silent.
But it is no less glorious.

God doesn't just heal to make you functional again.
He restores to reveal glory.
Your scars aren't shameful; they're proof of your becoming.
They're the stars in your procession.

You're not who you were.
And the world is beginning to notice.

INTERACTIVE REFLECTION

1. When was the last time you looked at yourself through God's eyes instead of shame's?
2. What does *radiance* mean to you? How does it feel when you carry quiet confidence rather than loud approval?
3. Can you name areas where God's light has begun to shine through your healing?

QUESTION AND ANSWER

Q: What if I still feel unsure and fragile? Does that mean I'm not radiant yet?

A: Radiance isn't about being invincible. It's about being real and rooted. Fragility doesn't cancel glory; it becomes the setting where His light shines brighter. The dawn doesn't rush, but it always rises.

SCRIPTURES FOR MEDITATION

"Those who look to Him are radiant; their faces are never covered with shame."
- Psalms 34:5 (NIV)

REFLECTIVE PROMPT

Write a letter from your future self, strong, radiant, free, to your present self. Let her speak life into you.

NOTES FROM MY JOURNAL

This morning, I didn't rush past the mirror.
I stood still.
Not to fix my face, but to finally see it.

I whispered to the woman staring back at me,
"You're still here."

Not because everything is perfect
But because I survived what should've taken me out.

Today, I didn't wear strength like a mask.
I wore it like a testimony.

The mirror didn't mock me.

It bore witness.

To my rising.

To my radiance.

To grace that met me in the quiet.

And for once, I believed it.

MY REFLECTION NOTES

(Use this space to write your thoughts, prayers, or what stood out to you today.)

_____

_____

_____

_____

_____

Date: _____

Thoughts & Impressions

_____

_____

_____

_____

_____

PRAYER

Lord,

Thank You for the light that rises even when I feel small.

Thank You for calling me radiant, even before I see it.

Teach me to walk with grace, to carry glory quietly, and to reflect Your beauty in broken places.

May I no longer fear the mirror. May I no longer hide behind old labels.

I am Yours. And You say I shine.

Amen.

DAY 18

WHEN HIS SILENCE SLIPPED

SCRIPTURES

"Surely the darkness will hide me and the light become night around me, yet even the darkness is not dark to You."
- **Psalms 139:11–12 (NIV)**

"Like a lily among thorns is my beloved among the daughters."
- **Songs of Solomon 2:2 (AMP)**

STORY REFLECTION: CHUCK'S QUIET COLLAPSE

Chuck sang in the choir.

A baritone that warmed the room, anchoring harmonies, ushering presence. His voice filled the sanctuary with strength even when his heart was empty.

To everyone else, he was fine.

He showed up on time. Smiled on cue. Wore his Sunday suit like armor. When he raised his hands during worship, no one could see how tightly they were clenched when he got home.

Debt.

Silence at home.

Pressure at work.

A wife who'd grown distant, tired of holding hope by herself. He couldn't say the words neither could he afford the fallout.

So, he swallowed them, week after week, and sang louder.

Until one rehearsal night.

He stayed behind, just for a moment. Sitting on the edge of the pew, staring at the cross like it owed him answers. His song had dried up somewhere between the bills and the shame.

That's when she walked in.

She wasn't looking for anyone. Just passing through. But something made her stop.

Maybe it was the way his shoulders slumped for the first time.

Maybe it was the echo of her own unraveling, not so long ago.

She sat beside him quietly. No small talk. Just presence.

"You okay?" She asked gently.

Chuck didn't answer.

Not at first.

He cleared his throat. Nodded.

But his voice betrayed him.

"I think I'm losing everything," he finally whispered. "And I don't know how to say it out loud without falling apart."

Her eyes softened. Not with pity, but with recognition.

"I used to think falling apart meant failure," she said. "Turns out, it was the first time I started healing."

Chuck didn't sob. He didn't collapse.

But a single tear broke through. And his silence—like hers once had—began to melt.

They sat there a while. No rush. No performance.

Just a man whose mask slipped. And a woman who saw him because she'd once been unseen.

And in the quiet of that empty sanctuary, healing began.

DEVOTIONAL THOUGHT

Many men wear a different kind of mask. Mask of silence. Mask of usefulness. Of performance. Of pretending not to feel.

Chuck's story reminds us: the weight of "holding it all together" is unsustainable for anyone. And sometimes, the most holy thing isn't to hold it in, but to let it fall.

God is not threatened by silence. He meets us there. Even in the dark places we think are too deep for rescue. He still comes close.

INTERACTIVE REFLECTION

1. Have you ever hidden behind silence, believing it was strength?
2. What would it look like to gently check in with the "strong ones" around you?
3. How would it feel to give yourself permission to speak, without editing?

QUESTION AND ANSWER

Q: Do I have to break down to be seen?

A: No, but you do have to be honest. God isn't moved by the volume of your pain; He's drawn to the authenticity of your surrender. You are safe to be seen.

SCRIPTURE FOR MEDITATION

- *"A bruised reed He will not break, and a faintly burning wick he will not quench; he will faithfully bring forth justice."* - **Isaiah 42:3. (NKJV).**

REFLECTIVE PROMPTS

- Write down what you wish someone had asked you when you were at your lowest.
- Who is someone you see carrying silent weight? How might you reach out?
- Reflect on a time your own mask slipped. What did it reveal and release?

NOTES FROM MY JOURNAL

I used to think silence was strength.
Now I know it can also be a slow surrender to shame.
When I heard Chuck's story, I remembered...
Masks don't always fall with a crash.
Sometimes, they melt in tears.
And that, too, is holy ground.

MY REFLECTION NOTES

(Use this space to write your thoughts, prayers, or what stood out to you today.)

_____
_____
_____
_____
_____

Date: _____

Thoughts & Impressions

_____

_____

_____

_____

_____

PRAYER

Jesus, thank You for not abandoning me in the ashes. Thank You for staying when others walked away. Teach me to lean on You, not just when I'm desperate, but when I'm healing. Turn my wilderness into a testimony. Let my life whisper of grace louder than any shame ever could. Amen.

DAY 19

THE VOICE THAT CALLED HER BY NAME

SCRIPTURE

"I will betroth you to Me forever; I will betroth you to Me in righteousness and justice, in love and compassion. I will betroth you to Me in faithfulness, and you will acknowledge the Lord."
- **Hosea 2:19-20 (NIV)**

"Arise, my love, my beautiful one, and come away."
- **Songs of Solomon 2:13b (AMP)**

"I have called you by name; you are mine."
- **Isaiah 43:1b (NLT)**

STORY REFLECTION: AFTER THE FINAL AMEN

It was an ordinary morning. The sun had barely risen, and the soft light trickled through the blinds, casting shadows across the living room. She was already up, getting the kids ready for school, packing lunches, making sure they remembered their homework. Her husband, still recovering, was slowly finding his rhythm again, no longer distant and tired. He smiled as she walked past him, a look of gratitude on his face, for her care, for the space she'd created for him to heal.

She moved through her day like she had countless others, getting the children settled, driving them off to school, managing household chores, making breakfast. There was always something else to do: the calls, the errands, the responsibilities.

But today was different.

It wasn't the rush of her morning routine that caught her attention. It was the quiet whisper in the middle of it all.

She had just finished packing a lunch when it came, soft, almost like a thought crossing her mind, but not quite.

"Beloved."

It was as if time paused. The noise around her, the bustle of daily life faded into the background. She stood still in the middle of the kitchen, feeling the weight of the world hang in the air. For a moment, she wondered if she had imagined it. She glanced at her husband, who was sipping his tea with his usual quiet contemplation. He didn't notice, didn't interrupt.

"Beloved," He repeated. And this time, it was unmistakable.

Not "wife." Not "mother." Not even "servant" Just............ "Beloved."

The same name He had whispered over her in quiet moments years ago, before the burdens of life had weighed her down. Before the shame of her past and the wounds of her soul had taken center stage.

She couldn't help but wonder: Did He really mean it? Was He still talking to her like that?

But as the thoughts swirled in her head, she began to breathe deeper, sensing a peace filling her that had been absent for so long. She wasn't just going through the motions of her day. She wasn't just a mother or a wife or a worker anymore. She was loved.

And something else lingered: Chuck's story.

She hadn't planned to carry his pain. But when his mask slipped, and his silence cracked, she had been there. Sat beside him. Heard the unsaid. Held his confession like something holy. And in doing so, something in her had shifted too.

She hadn't just helped Chuck.

She had helped herself.

She had remembered how much it meant to be seen. How sacred it was to be called out of silence.

That morning, as she stirred her tea, she smiled. Not out of pride, but purpose. The God who whispered *Beloved* into her chaos had used her voice to echo that same word into someone else's wilderness.

Her husband caught her eye then, a knowing smile spreading across his face. He was healing, slowly, but surely, and with every passing day, he was beginning to understand her strength, her love for him. It wasn't just the act of caregiving; it was the way she gave herself over to him, as she had to God. She had served with a heart of sacrifice, even when it felt like she was invisible. But now, there was something different in the way she moved in the world.

She went on with her day, getting herself ready for work, organizing the kids' things, the typical dance of life. But today, the quiet whisper of God's voice stayed with her.

As she got into the car to head to work, the words echoed again in her heart: "You are Mine."

And with those words, she walked through her day with renewed strength. She attended her meetings, reached out to her co-workers with kindness, and moved through her responsibilities with grace. Even when she went to church that evening, there was a new spark in her, a fervor she hadn't realized she'd lost.

She wasn't invisible anymore.

She was beloved.

DEVOTIONAL THOUGHT

We often lose ourselves in service, in roles, in responsibilities. We forget that we are not what we do; we are who we are called by.

And when He calls us *Beloved*, it is not because we've earned it. It's because He never stopped seeing us, even when we disappeared into our own routines.

When you step into someone else's pain and speak hope, you're not just rescuing them; you're remembering yourself.

INTERACTIVE REFLECTION

1. When was the last time you felt truly seen by God or someone else?
2. What name or label have you allowed to define you more than *Beloved*?
3. Is there someone whose story has reminded you of your own? How did that connection stir something sacred in you?

QUESTION AND ANSWER

Q: Can purpose come from ordinary days and quiet acts of love?

A: Yes. Purpose is often whispered, not shouted. It's found in the moments we don't post, the lives we touch quietly, the names God calls us when no one else is listening.

SCRIPTURE FOR MEDITATION

- *"The gatekeeper opens the gate for him, and the sheep listen to his voice. He calls his own sheep by name and leads them out."*
  - **John 10:3. (NIV).**

REFLECTIVE PROMPTS

- Write down the names you've called yourself this year. Then cross them out and write: *Beloved.*
- Reflect on someone whose healing reminded you of your own.
- Where is God calling you to remember your name?

NOTES FROM MY JOURNAL

Today, He didn't call me by title. He called me by truth. Beloved.

And in that word, I found myself again, not in the strength I give, but in the love I live.

Even in the kitchen. Even in the quiet. Even when I forget, He never does.

MY REFLECTION NOTES

(Use this space to write your thoughts, prayers, or what stood out to you today.)

_____
_____
_____
_____
_____

Date: _____

Thoughts & Impressions

_____

_____

_____

_____

_____

PRAYER

Father, thank You for calling me by name, not the name life gave me, but the one You gave me. Thank You for whispering *Beloved* into my ordinariness.

Help me to listen, even when the noise is loud. Help me to rest in my identity, even when I'm busy serving. Thank You for letting my voice echo healing in someone else's life and for reminding me that in loving them, I remember myself.

You see me. You name me. You love me. And I am Yours.

Amen.

DAY 20

THE BLOOMING CONTINUES

SCRIPTURES

"I will betroth you to Me forever; Yes, I will betroth you to Me in righteousness and justice, in lovingkindness and mercy; I will betroth you to Me in faithfulness, and you shall know the Lord."
- **Hosea 2:19-20. (NKJV).**

"How delightful is your love, my sister, my bride! How much more delightful is your love than wine, and the fragrance of your perfume more than any spice!"
- **Songs of Solomon 4:10. (NKJV).**

STORY REFLECTION: SHE BLOOMED; HE PAINTED

The mornings had become sacred again.

The sun still crept in slowly, brushing golden light across the kitchen floor, but something had shifted. What used to be heaviness, unpaid bills, silent prayers, weary bones, had begun to lift. Not because the world was suddenly perfect, but because she had changed.

There was rhythm now. Grace in the hustle. Purpose in the routine.

She moved through her home like a woman anchored, greeting her children not with stress, but with softness. Their laughter met her at the hallway, and instead of rushing, she paused. She kissed foreheads, tied shoelaces, and whispered prayers over backpacks, not as a chore, but as worship.

Her husband, once frail and fading into quiet despair, had found his rhythm again. He was painting.

Not just for escape, but for life. The easel returned to the corner of the sunlit room. The brush in his hand no longer trembled. The colors he chose were no longer muted. His first canvas in months carried swirls of joy, streaks of light and hope.

It was healing, on linen and in spirit.

He saw her now, not just as the caregiver, but as his companion in restoration. His muse, even. A woman whose steadiness had steadied him. And when he kissed her forehead that morning and said, "Have a good day, love," it held something weightier than routine; it carried reverence.

She smiled back. Not the tired smile of someone surviving, but the radiant one of someone becoming.

The drive to work was the same. But she was not. She no longer used it to rehearse worries or hold silent tears. Instead, she turned up her worship, rolled down the windows, and let the wind remind her: *You made it through. And you're still making it.*

At work, she walked with a steady grace. Her words were seasoned. Her presence disarmed tension. She no longer fought to prove her worth. She embodied it.

That evening, church didn't feel like a place to hide or plead. It felt like home. When she lifted her hands in worship, it wasn't to beg for rescue; it was to return thanks. Her voice was bold, her spirit open. There was no more shame echoing in her prayers. Only delight. Only Him.

"How delightful is your love………" the words from Songs of Solomon whispered through her heart like oil, sweet, fragrant, affirming. She wasn't just a woman restored. She was a bride. A beloved. Seen. Known. Desired by the One who never stopped calling her His.

And as her husband returned home that night with streaks of color on his hands and joy in his voice, she knew: this was what restoration looked like two hearts rising again, side by side.

DEVOTIONAL THOUGHT

There's a kind of freedom that isn't loud. It's quiet, steady and sacred.

It's the kind of freedom that lets you move through your routines with grace instead of grief. It shows up in the softness of your smile, in the strength that no longer needs to be explained.

God doesn't just rescue us to survive; He restores us to radiate. When the shame lifts and the healing begins, worship turns from a plea into a dance. You begin to live like you know you're loved.

You begin to bloom in your ordinariness.

INTERACTIVE REFLECTION

1. What daily routines once felt heavy but now feel lighter? Why?
2. Where in your day can you pause, not out of exhaustion, but to savor grace?
3. What would it mean to move through life as someone God delights in?

QUESTION AND ANSWER

Q: Do I have to wait until everything is perfect to feel free?

A: No. Freedom begins not when your world changes, but when your perspective does. God's love doesn't wait for perfection. It meets you in the middle of the mess and calls you radiant anyway.

SCRIPTURE FOR MEDITATION

- *"The Lord your God is in your midst, a mighty One who will save; He will rejoice over you with gladness; He will quiet you by His love; He will exult over you with loud singing."* - **Zephaniah 3:17. (NKJV).**

REFLECTIVE PROMPTS

- Where are you seeing signs of healing in your everyday life?
- Write about a moment this week that felt "ordinary" but was actually sacred.
- What is God whispering to you in this season of soft restoration?

NOTES FROM MY JOURNAL

Today felt light.
Not because everything's fixed, but because I've stopped fighting to be enough.

I tied shoelaces. I made breakfast. I folded laundry.
But none of it was routine. It was worship.

I'm not performing anymore.
I'm just... showing up.
Whole. His. Here.

MY REFLECTION NOTES

(Use this space to write your thoughts, prayers, or what stood out to you today.)

_____
_____
_____
_____
_____

Date: _____

Thoughts & Impressions

_____
_____
_____
_____
_____

PRAYER

Father, thank You for calling me to Yourself, for making me Your bride in righteousness, faithfulness, and mercy. I surrender my daily life to You. Every task, every interaction, every quiet moment. Help me to see the beauty in the routine and to live with purpose, knowing that my life is an offering to You. May the fragrance of my love for You fill every space I walk into in Jesus' name, Amen.

DAY 21

THE DANCE OF THE REDEEMED

SCRIPTURE

> *"Who is this that appears like the dawn, fair as the moon, bright as the sun, majestic as the stars in procession?"*
> - **Song**s **of Solomon 6:10. (ESV).**

STORY REFLECTION: THE POSTURE OF BECOMING

She sat with her colleagues in the boardroom, surrounded by whiteboards, notes, and strategic language, *"funneling," "deep diving," "positioning."* Voices overlapped, graphs changed, and decisions were drawn like arrows across flip charts. She didn't need to lead the room. She didn't even need to speak often.

She just sat, steady. With a soft smile that came not from arrogance but peace.

She contributed with wisdom when it counted. And when she didn't speak, her stillness held weight. She wasn't rushing to be impressive. She wasn't shrinking either. She had learned to let her presence speak when her words didn't need to.

No one else noticed the shift, but she did. The old her would've over-explained, tried too hard, measured her value by response. But not today.

Today, she knew who she was.

Later, after the meeting, she lingered for a moment, tucking her notes slowly, breathing in the rhythm of a life that had finally quieted. When she returned to her desk, she stood by the window for a moment, tea in hand. The sun spilled gently across the floor, and she remembered mornings past. The chaos. The questions. The desperate prayers.

But that was before.
Before the healing.
Before the masks fell.
Before she believed she could be loved without proving it.

She had done this morning routine a thousand times, blessing her children out the door, smoothing her husband's now-steady hands, whispering prayers over her home. But now, her posture had shifted. Her steps were no longer weighed down by guilt or anxiety.

She didn't carry shame anymore.
She carried *grace*.
And it held her without rush. Without pressure. Without performance.

She thought of the woman who'd come into her office the week before, tired, quiet, searching for a reason not to quit. She had seen the signs, remembered that ache. But now, she didn't need to fix her. Just to sit. To share. To say, "Me too."

And in that simple exchange, something holy passed between them: truth, presence, permission to hope again.

From the window, she looked down at the people below. The city hadn't changed. But she had.

And as she turned away, she heard it, not from a speaker, but from the hush within:

"You are majestic in your rising. You are radiant. You are Mine."

She didn't need to speak it aloud.
She already believed it.

DEVOTIONAL THOUGHT

There is strength in showing up without striving.

There is a shift that happens when your inner posture changes, when you stop bracing for rejection and start resting in your belovedness.

You don't need to be loud to lead. You don't need to be noticed to matter.

You are becoming more radiant, not because of what you do, but because of *who you now know you are.*

This is the posture of becoming.
Still. Steady. Holy.

INTERACTIVE REFLECTION

1. How has your posture shifted in this season: emotionally, spiritually, physically?
2. What pressure have you been released from recently?
3. Who around you might be waiting for your quiet "me too"?

QUESTION AND ANSWER:

Q: Can I really carry healing without needing a spotlight?

A: Yes. Your presence, your peace, your quiet honesty, these are powerful. You don't have to be public to be purposeful. God uses those who are simply *willing to be.*

SCRIPTURE FOR MEDITATION

"Those who look to Him are radiant and their faces shall never be ashamed"
- Psalms 34:5. (NKJV).

REFLECTIVE PROMPTS

- What has changed about the way you enter a room or conversation lately?
- Write a note to yourself celebrating how far you've come, even if no one else sees it.
- Who are you becoming when no one is watching?

NOTES FROM MY JOURNAL

I didn't say much in today's meeting.

But I didn't need to.

Peace doesn't need volume.
And sometimes, healing looks like sitting at the table: unshaken, unseen… but whole.

MY REFLECTION NOTES

(Use this space to write your thoughts, prayers, or what stood out to you today.)

_____
_____
_____
_____
_____

Date: _____

Thoughts & Impressions

_____

_____

_____

_____

_____

PRAYER

Father, thank You for the transformation You are working in me. I no longer walk in shame, but in the brilliance of Your redemption. Help me carry the light of my healing to others. Teach me to dance in the radiance of grace, to shine like the dawn, and to never forget the One who walked me out of darkness. Use my story, Lord. Let it sing of Your faithfulness in Jesus' name, Amen.

DAY 22

THE FRAGRANCE SURRENDER

SCRIPTURE

"Your name is like perfume poured out.
No wonder the young women love you."
- **Songs of Solomon 1:3. (ESV).**

STORY REFLECTION: THE SCENT THAT STAYED

She never imagined healing would have a scent.

It started quietly, like most holy things do.

She was standing in line at the grocery store, distracted by her list and half-worried about making it to the school pickup line on time. That's when it happened.

A soft tap on her shoulder.

"Excuse me," the woman behind her said, hesitant. "I know this might sound strange but………., are you wearing something? A scent? It's comforting, familiar."

She blinked. At first, confused. She hadn't worn perfume in weeks, maybe months. But then, like a whisper from memory, she remembered that morning.

Knees bent beside her bed.
Tears that weren't from pain anymore, but from awe.
She had poured her soul out like oil before the Lord, raw, quiet, emptied.

And somehow, something had poured back in.

Not loud. Not dramatic. Just peace. Stillness. Presence.

THE MASK SHE WORE: THE REBIRTH MADELINE AGOBA

A fragrance not from a bottle, but from a posture.

She remembered the early days of healing, when silence still scared her and joy felt like a language she had forgotten. But now? Now it clung to her like grace. And others could sense it, even when she wasn't trying.

In the church hallway, someone paused mid-conversation.
"You feel like peace," they whispered.

At work, a colleague lingered after a strategy meeting, eyes tired, voice low.
"You remind me that all is not lost," he said.
She hadn't spoken a word.

It wasn't her voice. It was her *presence*.

It was in the way she moved through rooms now with ease, not fear.
The way she laughed, not guarded, but full.
The way her silence didn't beg for attention anymore; it *blessed* it.

She remembered when everything about her had reeked of desperation.
The stale scent of debts.
The fog of shame that clung like heavy perfume.
She had tried to scrub it off with performance, with praise, with pretty distractions and heavy perfumes.

But none of it lasted.

Until *He* poured Himself into the cracked alabaster of her life.

And now, the scent lingered.

That morning, while braiding her daughter's hair, her little girl looked up suddenly and said, "Mummy, you smell like love."

She paused, her hand frozen in mid-braid.

Tears gathered, soft and sacred.

It was not perfume.
It was *Presence*.

The fragrance of redemption.
The aroma of healing.
The name of her Beloved, poured out across every ordinary corner of her days.

DEVOTIONAL THOUGHT

There is a fragrance to healing, not always detectable by the world, but unmistakable to the weary.

You may not realize it, but the peace you now carry is speaking. Not loudly. Not forcefully. But steadily like incense rising from a life once broken, now whole.

The name of Jesus, poured out over your cracks, leaves a lingering scent.

It's not in what you wear or what you say.
It's in who you've become.
And those around you, hurting, aching, waiting, can smell the grace.

Let your life pour.

INTERACTIVE REFLECTION

1. Has anyone ever told you that they feel safe or calm around you? How did it make you feel?
2. What used to cling to you that no longer defines you?
3. In what ways has your atmosphere shifted since you began healing?

QUESTION AND ANSWER

Q: What if I feel like my life doesn't smell like redemption yet?

A: Scents settle over time. The oil of His presence may not be obvious to you right now, but as you continue to yield and heal, your life will carry it. Even your quiet moments are steeped in His fragrance.

SCRIPTURES FOR MEDITATION

- Psalm 45:8 - *"All your robes are fragrant with myrrh and aloes and cassia............... ". (ESV).*
- Songs of Solomon 4:11 - *"Your lips drip nectar, my bride; honey and milk are under your tongue; The fragrance of your garments is like the fragrance of Lebanon." (ESV).*

REFLECTIVE PROMPTS

- Write about the "fragrance" your life used to carry and the one you long to carry now.
- Think of someone whose presence has been a balm to you. What did they carry?
- What does "smelling like love" mean to you?

NOTES FROM MY JOURNAL

I used to carry the scent of desperation.
Now people say I smell like hope.
I didn't notice the shift.
But heaven did.
And that's enough.

MY REFLECTION NOTES

(Use this space to write your thoughts, prayers, or what stood out to you today.)

_____
_____
_____
_____
_____

Date: _____

Thoughts & Impressions

_____
_____
_____
_____
_____

PRAYER

Lord, I never imagined You could turn my ashes into a fragrance. But You did. Thank You for making my life a sweet-smelling offering. May my presence always reflect Yours. Let Your name be the oil that pours through my every interaction, my silence, my story, my scars. Make my life a garden of grace. And let the world inhale Your love through me. Amen.

DAY 23

THE GARDEN KEEPER

SCRIPTURE

"You who dwell in the gardens with friends in attendance, let me hear your voice."
- **Songs of Solomon 8:13. (ESV).**

STORY REFLECTION: THE GARDEN SHE NOW TENDED

She stood barefoot in the backyard, the morning sun spilling across the lawn like warm oil. Her husband had gone for his morning walk, a new rhythm he'd adopted since the bloom and since healing found its way back into their home. The kids were still asleep. It was Saturday, her sacred pause.

She knelt beside the planter boxes she had built herself, lavender, mint, basil, plants she had learned to care for. Not just because they were fragrant and useful, but because nurturing them reminded her to nurture herself.

Each one had nearly died when she first planted them. Their stems were fragile. Their roots uncertain. Like her. But with steady watering, warmth, and patience, they had flourished.

The quiet hum of the morning wrapped around her like a shawl. She wiped her hands on her cotton robe and glanced toward the patio table where her journal sat open, pages filled with ink and tears, worship and wondering. There were scribbles from her daughter, and on the corners of the page, fingerprints from grace. Every prayer etched inside reminded her: her voice had once been buried beneath shame. But not anymore.

Once, she was the woman who kept quiet in rooms full of noise. Not because she had nothing to say, but because she feared her truth would scatter people.

Now, she was the keeper of gardens. And her voice had become shelter.

She mentored younger women, some from church, others from work, and many more who found her in the quiet corners of social media. They came to her, not for sermons, but for sanctuary. Not for perfection, but peace.

She rarely gave answers. She gave presence. And when she did speak, her voice didn't rise with performance; it flowed with wisdom.

"You're not a failure," she told one just last night.
"To bloom again isn't betrayal," she'd reminded another.
And to herself:
"You are not who you were. But you needed her to become this."

She had become a safe place. A quiet garden. A living altar.

And the One who had always seen her, the One who walked with her through storms and silence, still came close.

"Let me hear your voice," he whispered in the quiet hush of that morning.

So, she responded. Not with eloquence. Not with performance

She didn't sing. She didn't weep. She simply hummed, low and steady, as she watered a plant that had once nearly died.

And there, in the glow of morning light, with no makeup, no audience, and no titles, she worshiped.

She was no longer hiding.

She was blooming.
She was rooted.
She was home.

DEVOTIONAL THOUGHT

There's sacredness to tending what once withered.

When you've walked through fire and still choose to garden, still choose beauty, still offer grace, you become a living testament. Your life speaks even when your mouth is quiet.

God delights in your growth. But more than that, He delights in your *voice*, not your polished speech, but the real, raw melody that rises when you realize you are no longer surviving. You're flourishing.

And He still walks in the garden of your soul.

INTERACTIVE REFLECTION

1. What garden in your life are you being called to tend?
2. Have you become a place of peace for others? How has that journey looked?
3. When was the last time you truly believed your voice mattered to God?

QUESTION AND ANSWER

Q: What if I don't feel ready to mentor or pour into others yet?

A: You don't have to be "ready." You only have to be *present*. Your story in process still carries power. Sometimes, the garden others need is just the proof that growth is possible.

SCRIPTURE FOR MEDITATION

- *"Awake, o North wind, and come, o South wind! Blow upon my garden, let its spices flow. Let my beloved come into his garden and eat its choicest fruits."* - **Songs of Solomon 4:16. (ESV).**

REFLECTIVE PROMPTS

- Write about what your "garden" looks like today, what you're cultivating, pruning, watering.
- List three people who've found rest or reflection in your presence.
- Ask yourself: What does God delight to hear from me today?

NOTES FROM MY JOURNAL

I didn't realize I had become someone's shade.
But now I see the pain that once scorched me made room for others to rest.

He walks in my garden still.
And He calls me by my voice, not my perfection.

MY REFLECTION NOTES

(Use this space to write your thoughts, prayers, or what stood out to you today.)

_____
_____
_____
_____
_____

Date: _____

Thoughts & Impressions

_____

_____

_____

_____

_____

PRAYER

Father, thank You for restoring, not just my soul, but my sound. I didn't know I would ever speak again, not without shame, not without pain. But here I am, in the garden You planted, and my voice has become a song. Help me to steward it well. Let my words water dry hearts. Let my life carry the fragrance of Your presence. And in every whisper, let it be You they hear. Amen.

DAY 24

WHEN SILENCE SPOKE THE LOUDEST

SCRIPTURE

> *"Your shoots are an orchard of pomegranates with choice fruits............"*
> **- Songs of Solomon 4:13. (ESV).**

STORY REFLECTION: WHEN HER PRESENCE BEGAN TO PREACH LOUDER THAN HER PAST

She knew what it meant to be trusted, gifted, and *still quietly stretched*.

To be the one others called when they needed prayer, counsel, or encouragement
while silently working the numbers in her head, ensuring nothing slipped through the cracks.

She never let the wear show.
Not when she walked into boardrooms.
Not when she stood before a congregation.
Not even when she was home, folding laundry and managing everything from school fees to meal plans, with a smile that had become both her strength and her shield.

She didn't live in lack, but *she knew the tension*.
The pressure of having *just enough*, but not enough margin to breathe.
The careful calculating, the quiet substitutions, the holy discipline of stretching what others didn't realize needed stretching.

She was not poor in purpose.

She was rich in faith.
But sometimes, the numbers simply didn't align with the vision.

And yet, she kept pouring.
Kept sowing.
Kept showing up faithful in the quiet places where no applause echoed.

There were days she watched others soar ahead, with less sacrifice and more applause.
She congratulated them with grace. But sometimes, in the solitude of her night prayers, she'd whisper:
"Lord, have You forgotten me?"

But He hadn't.

Healing came slowly like morning light slipping through a drawn curtain.
Not dramatic. Not loud. But steady. Certain. Transformational.
And as the fog of pressure lifted and the old whispers of shame lost their volume,
she didn't simply rise.

She *turned back*.

Not to wallow in what was, but to *open the kind of door she had once needed*.

Because now, she saw them too.

Women who were smart and sometimes, anointed but silently weighed down by invisible ceilings.
They weren't lazy. They weren't useless.
They were the economically empowered poor women who had potential, ideas, and strength, but lacked structure, access, and someone who saw beyond the polish.

They were the ones society had forgotten.
The ones who once begged for scraps, and were handed them without dignity.
The ones whose eyes no one looked into anymore.
But she looked.
And she saw.

So, she began to build.

Not just words. Not just prayers.
Platforms. Pathways. Purpose.

She helped them see themselves as more than survivors.
She reminded them they were not forgotten, they were useful, dignified, still deeply needed.

She sat with them.
Registered ideas with them.
Laid out business plans on kitchen tables.
Taught them how to price their work without apology.
How to turn hobbies into income.
How to keep their eyes on their children and their hands on their purpose.

She didn't just empower them; she provoked their dignity.

Because she knew what it meant to feel capable and overlooked.
And now?
She wasn't just surviving.
She was multiplying hope.

DEVOTIONAL THOUGHT

Sometimes, the greatest proof of your healing is not your personal peace; it's the *harvest of others* who walk through a door you chose to hold open.

We often imagine fruitfulness as something measured in accolades or applause.

But heaven measures differently.

Heaven sees the lives changed because you said "yes" after your own "almost."

You are not just a vessel of healing; you are a builder of futures.

INTERACTIVE REFLECTION

1. Who in your world is quietly stretched, silently faithful, and waiting for one open door?
2. What practical steps can you take this month to become a door for someone else?
3. What "little" seed do you carry that could be someone else's breakthrough?

QUESTION AND ANSWER

Q: What if I don't feel ready to help someone else yet?

A: You don't need to have "arrived" to open a door. You just need to be willing. Sometimes, it's your in-process honesty, not perfection, that sets another soul free.

SCRIPTURES FOR MEDITATION

- *"And your ancient ruins shall be rebuilt; you shall raise up the foundations of many generations; you shall be called the repairer of the breach, the restorer of streets to dwell in."* - **Isaiah 58:12. (NKJV).**
- *"She opens her arms to the poor and extends her hands to the needy."* - **Proverbs 31:20. (NKJV).**

REFLECTIVE PROMPTS

- List the names of two women (or men) you feel led to support, empower, or encourage in this season.
- Reflect on what you've built with little and how that qualifies you to help others do the same.
- Write out one dream you laid down due to limitation. Could it be time to revisit it now, for others?

NOTES FROM MY JOURNAL

I used to whisper, *"God, if You bring me through, I'll reach back."*
Now I see why He let me feel the tension.
Why He allowed me to walk with both oil and limitation.
So I'd know how to hold the door *without judgment.*
And hand others the keys *with grace.*

MY REFLECTION NOTES

(Use this space to write your thoughts, prayers, or what stood out to you today.)

_____
_____
_____
_____
_____

Date: _____

Thoughts & Impressions

_____

_____

_____

_____

_____

PRAYER

Father,

Thank You for trusting me with the stretch and the strength.

For showing me that healing isn't just for wholeness; it's for harvest.

Make me generous, discerning, and faithful in the small.

Use my hands, my scars, and my journey as tools for someone else's freedom.

Let my life become a doorway to possibility, restoration, and dignity.

In Jesus' Name,
Amen.

DAY 25

A MIRROR NAMED MIRIAM

SCRIPTURES

> *"Let me see your face, let me hear your voice;*
> *for your voice is sweet and your face is lovely."*
> **- Songs of Solomon 2:14. (ESV).**

> *"They will be called oaks of righteousness,*
> *a planting of the Lord for the display of His splendor.*
> *They will rebuild the ancient ruins........."*
> **- Isaiah 61:3-4. (ESV)**

STORY REFLECTION: SEEING HER REFLECTION IN ANOTHER'S TEARS

She wasn't expecting her that day.

It was a warm Thursday afternoon. The sun spilled gently through the church hall's long windows, dancing across the worn wooden floor as she adjusted chairs for the women's study group she now mentored.

It was still surreal to think that she, once hiding behind perfection, pain, shame and brokenness; now stood in front of women with a Bible in her hand and a healed story in her heart.

That's when she saw her: Miriam.
Timid. Head bowed. Clothes too carefully chosen to conceal how small she felt inside. There was something familiar in her gait. A silent scream behind her soft "hello."

She didn't press. She simply offered her the seat beside her. And slowly, over weeks, Miriam began to exhale.

It started with casual comments about being tired. Then came the teary laughter. The "me too" moments. The confession that she hadn't prayed in months. That she felt like a fraud every time she came to church. That the weight of an ill husband, four restless teenagers, and unpaid bills had left her brittle and bitter.

That she had once loved God passionately but now felt like a forgotten name in His registry.

She listened fully. Without judgment. Without performance. Because she had been Miriam. She *was* Miriam, just a few steps ahead.

One evening after study, Miriam lingered. Her voice cracked: "How do you keep going?"

The answer flowed without a script:
"Because He never let me go. Even when I let Him go."

That night, she told Miriam her story. Not the edited version, but the raw one. The one with nights she thought of walking away from everything. The one where debt wrapped shame like a second skin. The one where she once hated the very people she smiled for. The one where healing didn't come in a day but came anyway.

Miriam wept.

And in those tears, a door creaked open in her heart.
Later that week, a message came:
"You made me believe He could still want me. That I wasn't too messed up to be seen as beautiful again."

It wrecked her in the best way.

Now she saw it clearly. This healing was never just hers to keep.
It was a key for others.
Her brokenness, now mended, had become a map.

Her wounds, now kissed by grace, had become a witness.
Her voice, once silenced by shame, had become a song someone else needed to hear.

DEVOTIONAL THOUGHT

You may think your story is too scarred to be of any use, but someone else is waiting to see their reflection in your survival.

Miriam represents every woman (and man) who sits silently in pain, waiting for someone real. Not perfect, but real. Someone whose story says, "Me too, and here's how I made it through." You don't need a platform to help others heal. Just presence, honesty, and your testimony: unpolished and true.

Your healing is not the end of your story.
It is the door for someone else's beginning.

INTERACTIVE REFLECTION

1. Who has been a "Miriam" in your life, someone you recognized because you've lived her pain?
2. Have you ever hesitated to share your story out of fear of being too messy or too real?
3. Who might need your story right now, not your perfection, but your presence?

QUESTION AND ANSWER

Q: Can my story really help someone else, even if I'm still healing?

A: Yes. You don't need to be completely whole to be useful. You only need to be open. Even cracked vessels carry water. Your honesty may be the healing someone else has been praying for.

SCRIPTURES FOR MEDITATION

- *"Blessed be the God and Father of our Lord Jesus Christ, the Father of mercies and God of all comfort. Who comforts us in all our afflictions, so that we may be able to comfort those who are in any affliction, with the comfort with which we ourselves are comforted by God."* - **2 Corinthians 1:3-4. (NKJV).**
- *"Let the redeemed of the Lord tell their story, whom He has redeemed from trouble."* - **Psalms 107:2. (NKJV).**

REFLECTIVE PROMPTS

- Write a short letter to a younger version of yourself, the one who needed to know healing was possible.
- Make a list of 3 truths your story now carries that could free someone else.
- Reach out to someone who reminds you of your "before." Ask how they're really doing.

NOTES FROM MY JOURNAL

I didn't plan to share the unedited version.

But then she sat beside me, wide-eyed, weary, and so much like I once was.

In her tears, I recognized my old silence.

In her questions, I heard my past echo.

I spoke, not from perfection, but from the path I'd walked.

Healing wasn't just for me.

It was a doorway for her too.

Maybe that's the point.

My healed voice becomes someone else's lifeline.

My story, a mirror showing her: You're not too far gone.

Not forgotten. Not forsaken. Just found, again.

MY REFLECTION NOTES

(Use this space to write your thoughts, prayers, or what stood out to you today.)

Date: _____

Thoughts & Impressions

PRAYER

Father,

Thank You for entrusting me with healing, and with others.

Help me not to hide what You've redeemed.

Let my story be a seed in the soil of another woman's (or man's) breakthrough.

Let me see those around me not as burdens, but as mirrors, reminders of what You've brought me through.

I open my mouth, Lord, not to impress, but to bless.

Use me. Even in my unfinished places.

Amen.

DAY 26

WHEN GRACE CARRIED WHAT GUILT COVERED

SCRIPTURES

> *"By the grace of God I am what I am, and His grace to me was not without effect."*
> **- 1 Corinthians 15:10. (NKJV).**

> *"You are beautiful, my darling, as Tirzah, lovely as Jerusalem, majestic as troops with banners."*
> **- Song of Solomon 6:4. (NKJV).**

STORY REFLECTION: WHERE MINISTRY MET SHAME AND MERCY STILL ANSWERED

He was known for miracles.
A healing evangelist. Revered. Traveled the world with power and signs. People lined up for prayer, for breakthrough, for the touch of the anointed.

But back home sat his daughter.
Curled feet. Born with a deformity.
And every night, while he prayed for others, he laid hands on her too.
Nothing changed.

He never stopped loving. He never stopped praying. But inside, he wrestled with the ache that no one else could see. How do you keep healing others while your own child remains untouched? How do you keep the miracles flowing when your own heart bleeds quietly?

He wore a mask, not of hypocrisy, but of survival.
Not of denial, but of devotion.

Until one day, as he worshiped in silence after another full crusade, he heard it:

"You can seek help and still trust Me."

And for the first time, he wept openly, raw, in surrender.

It wasn't a lack of faith. It was an act of wisdom.
He flew his daughter out for surgery.
And in time, she walked into a room he once couldn't carry her into.

But he never forgot that season.
The one where his strength was shaped not on the stage, but in the silence.

ADA'S STORY: THE GRACE SHE NEVER POSTED

To the world, Ada was poised, refined, and fiercely admirable.

She was elegance in motion, the kind of woman people quoted, reposted, and invited to speak on "becoming" and "healing." Her online presence radiated balance: spirituality, sophistication, and just the right shade of vulnerable.

But behind the filters and quotes, was a silence she never dared to caption.

Years ago, in a different life, Ada had made a decision that followed her like shadow. A decision born not from rebellion, but from exhaustion. Her marriage had been crumbling for years, a slow, lonely unravelling. She had begged, prayed, and fasted until her ribs ached and her spirit wilted. But the love never returned.

And in one emotionally fragile night, in the arms of someone who *listened*, she made a choice she never imagined she would: adultery.

She carried it for months, thinking if she buried it beneath good works, it would die. It didn't. The truth came out. Her marriage ended. Her image shattered. Her faith community recoiled. Whispers followed her everywhere, even when she walked alone.

The shame was unbearable. So, she disappeared.

Rebuilt. Slowly. Quietly.

God never left. That's what stunned her most. Even when others did, He stayed. He didn't excuse her fall, but He didn't withhold His love either. Instead, He led her gently into restoration. Not the kind that glosses over sin, but the kind that confronts it, forgives it, and renews the whole soul.

Years passed. She remarried a good man. A kind man.
She began a new life, a new name, a new platform.
And with it, came a new mask.

It was subtle. Not lies, just silence.
She became the poster woman for restoration without ever saying *what* she had been restored from.

Until one day, after a panel discussion on "grace and grit," a woman approached her. Teary. Vulnerable.
"I don't think God can use me," she said. "I made a mistake. A big one. I crossed lines. I don't even recognize myself anymore."

Ada felt something cracked.

She reached for the woman's hand and whispered, "Me too."

That night, Ada went home and stared at her reflection.
She looked radiant but not free.

And she knew: it was time. Not to spill everything. Not to create spectacle. But to *stop hiding*.

So, in a quiet blog post, not tagged, not shared, just offered , she wrote:

"I made a mistake. But grace met me there. And that grace rebuilt me. Slowly. Tenderly. Completely."

She didn't tell the story to invite pity.

She told it to *set someone else free*.

DEVOTIONAL THOUGHT

Sometimes, the mask isn't about hiding pain; it's about hiding the journey.

We want to show the result, not the wrestle. The platform, not the process. The crown, not the cross that came first. And so, we rob others of the very thing they need most: our *realness*.

You don't have to be unfinished to tell your story.
But you also don't need to pretend that the becoming never happened.

Your vulnerability is not weakness.
It's a gift.

INTERACTIVE REFLECTION

1. Have you ever downplayed your becoming because you were afraid of looking messy?
2. Are there parts of your story you've hidden to maintain an image?
3. Who could your honesty set free today?

QUESTION AND ANSWER

Q: Isn't it better to protect people from my past and just inspire them with my now?

A: Inspiration without truth is hollow. Your *now* becomes more powerful when people understand the *how*. Let them see the cracks. That's where the light gets in.

SCRIPTURES FOR MEDITATION

- *"After you have suffered a little while, the God of all grace, who has called you into His eternal glory in Christ, will Himself restore, confirm, strengthen and establish you."* - **1 Peter 5:10. (NKJV).**
- *"Who is this who appears like the dawn… beautiful as the moon, majestic as the stars in procession?"* - **Song of Solomon 6:10. (ESV).**

REFLECTIVE PROMPTS

- Write down a part of your journey you've been afraid to share. Why?
- What would it look like to embrace that chapter as part of your strength?
- Who in your life needs to know that "becoming" is holy?

NOTES FROM MY JOURNAL

I didn't always want to tell my story.
I thought the mess disqualified the miracle.
But now I see, the miracle makes sense *because* of the mess.
I'm not here in spite of the journey.
I'm here *because* of it.

MY REFLECTION NOTES

(Use this space to write your thoughts, prayers, or what stood out to you today.)

_____
_____
_____
_____
_____

Date: _____

Thoughts & Impressions

_____
_____
_____
_____
_____

PRAYER

Father,

Thank You for the beauty of the becoming.

Thank You for grace in the quiet places, for the courage to rise without pretending.

Help me to be honest, not just about what You've done, but about how You did it.

Let my story be a bridge. Let my truth be a healing balm.

Let those who see me *know* You.

Amen.

DAY 27

THE RESCUE AT THE CROSSROADS

SCRIPTURES

"The Lord is my rock, my fortress and my deliverer; my God is my rock, in whom I take refuge."
- **Psalm 18:2 (NIV)**

"Arise, my love, my beautiful one, and come away."
- **Songs of Solomon 2:10b (NIV)**

STORY REFLECTION: WHEN BROKEN PATHS MEET REDEEMING HANDS

It was just a Wednesday.
The kind where the sky wore grey like a veil and the office lights flickered just enough to match the heaviness in the air.

She had gone in early, needing the quiet. But she wasn't the only one.

Lara was already there.

She sat curled on the far end of the breakroom couch, coffee cradled in trembling hands, eyes fixed on something far away. Always the first in, always the last out. Diligent. Smart. Invisible.

To most, Lara was the dependable one.
To the whispers around the office, she was "overworked" or "probably going through something."
But no one ever asked.

Until that morning.

As she poured her tea, she stole a glance at Lara. Something about the stillness of her shoulders struck her. It wasn't peace. It was resignation.

She paused.

Walked over slowly.

"Hey," she said gently, "Can I sit?"

Lara blinked. Didn't smile. But nodded.

Silence settled between them, thick as wool.
Then Lara whispered: "I'm so tired."

And the dam broke.
Not with sobs, but with a trembling confession:
Of crushing debt.
Of a boss who demanded perfection but offered no kindness.
Of a home filled with pressure from a husband who accused her of doing too much and still not being enough.
Of the loneliness of being "the strong one" everyone counted on but no one truly saw.

"I'm good at..... pretending," she stammered. "Most days, I wear it well. But today, I…..i…….just……….. can't."

And the listener's heart split open because she had worn that same armor.

She reached for Lara's hand, slow and sacred.

"I know that kind of tired," she whispered. "The kind where silence feels safer than honesty. I've been there, behind the mask, beneath the weight."

She didn't offer clichés or quick fixes. She shared her story, the one scarred with debt, silence, shame, and survival. She spoke of the

Voice that whispered *"Arise, my love"* when she thought she was too far gone to be wanted. Too broken to be useful.

Lara didn't say much. But her grip tightened. Her chin quivered.

And then came the tear.

Not loud, not dramatic. Just one holy drop that said: *I'm unraveling, and I don't want to do it alone.*

That's when she saw him, Chuck, standing by the coffee machine, pretending not to listen.

But his eyes gave him away.

The man who told the best jokes in the office. The one always "fine." The choir tenor. The husband who tried so hard to be everything his wife wanted and still came up short. The one who had taken on too much, stretched too thin, and now lived inside the echo of *"You're not enough."*

Their eyes met.

"I see you too," she said softly.

Chuck didn't move. But his shoulders dropped. His eyes glistened. The mask slipped.

And just like that, she understood:

This wasn't just about Lara. Or Chuck.
This was about *her healing becoming their invitation.*

God had turned her breakdown into a map.
Her silence into a song.
Her scars into safe places for others to be seen.

DEVOTIONAL THOUGHT

We all reach crossroads, places where we can't keep pretending, where our masks no longer protect, only suffocate.

Sometimes, God sends someone not to rescue us with answers, but to sit beside us in the unraveling.

And when we've walked through fire, our presence becomes proof that others can survive the heat too.

Your healing is not the end of the story. It's a beginning for someone else.

INTERACTIVE REFLECTION

1. Who around you is quietly drowning beneath a strong face?
2. When did someone's story unlock healing for you?
3. How might God use your journey to sit with another at their own crossroads?

QUESTION AND ANSWER

Q: I'm not a counselor or pastor. What can I possibly offer someone who's broken?

A: You offer what most people truly need: presence. Not sermons. Not solutions. Just presence. And that, friend, is sacred.

SCRIPTURES FOR MEDITATION

- *"When you pass through the waters, I will be with you."* - **Isaiah 43:2. (NKJV)**.
- *"Bear one another's burdens........"* - **Genesis 6:2. (NKJV)**
- *"Arise, come, my darling; my beautiful one, come with me."* - **Songs of Solomon 2:13. (NKJV)**.

REFLECTIVE PROMPTS

- Who have you quietly related to but never approached?
- What part of your story do you still hesitate to share and why?
- Write a letter (even if you never send it) to someone who once helped you breathe again.

NOTES FROM MY JOURNAL

Some days, rescue sounds like "I see you."
Other days, it's just sitting beside someone until they exhale.
Today, I didn't save anyone;
I simply stayed.

And God was in that.

MY REFLECTION NOTES

(Use this space to write your thoughts, prayers, or what stood out to you today.)

_____
_____
_____
_____
_____

Date: _____

Thoughts & Impressions

_____
_____
_____
_____
_____

> **PRAYER**
>
> Lord, thank You for giving me the strength to see others in their pain and to reach out with compassion. Help me to be a vessel of Your rescue, to offer a listening ear and gentle encouragement when someone feels forgotten. May my story, and the healing You have granted me, light the way for those still lost in darkness. Empower me to share Your love boldly, knowing that even in our brokenness. Your grace makes us whole. In Jesus' name, Amen.

INTERLUDE

DEBT IS NOT A SIN, BUT THE MASK MIGHT BE

It starts small.

A quiet "I'm fine" when everything inside is untangling.

A practiced smile.

A nod of strength while your knees are buckling beneath the surface.

You show up. You serve. You give.

And all the while, the weight deepens.

Not being able to meet financial demands is not a crime.

Debt is not a sin.

Heaven doesn't blacklist you for unpaid bills.

God is not ashamed of your lack.

But the mask……………………

The pressure to pretend, to perform, to protect your image……………

That's where the soul begins to crack.

The enemy knows it.

That's why he doesn't just tempt us with sin; he tempts us with appearances.

He teaches us to "fake it till you make it."

To bury our brokenness beneath curated captions and perfectly phrased prayers.

But here's the truth:

THE MASK SHE WORE: THE REBIRTH MADELINE AGOBA

The devil wears masks too.

He is the master deceiver.

He knows that as long as you hide, healing can't reach you.

As long as you perform, freedom will elude you.

Because what you conceal, God can't transform.

God doesn't bless your performance.

He blesses your presence.

Your honesty. Your surrender.

So here's the invitation, not to shame, but to stillness.

Come into The Sacred Hush.

That space where truth is safe.

Where masks fall and mercy speaks.

Where your lack is met with love,

And your cracks become the very place His light pours through.

Take off the weight.

Lay down the disguise.

There's no fear in being seen,

Not here.

Just hush.

And healing.

DAY 28

THE DAY THE DOORS OPENED

SCRIPTURES

> *"Defend the weak and the fatherless;*
> *uphold the cause of the poor and the oppressed."*
> **- Psalm 82:3 (NIV)**

> *"My dove in the clefts of the rock, in the hiding places on the mountainside, show me your face, let me hear your voice; for your voice is sweet, and your face is lovely."*
> **- Songs of Solomon 2:14 (NIV)**

STORY REFLECTION: WHEN COMPASSION BECAME A BRIDGE

It started with a simple "Are you OK?"
A question she almost didn't ask.
A door she almost didn't open.

Bible study had ended, and chairs were being stacked with the usual rhythm of fellowship winding down. But her eyes caught Chinny, again.

Always folding her shawl a little too slowly, as if the weight on her shoulders made even small movements heavy.
The Holy Spirit whispered urgently: *Don't look away this time.*

She crossed the room and touched Chinny's arm.
At first, Chinny tried to smile, tried to fake fine. But her lip trembled.
And then, quietly, she broke.

THE MASK SHE WORE: THE REBIRTH MADELINE AGOBA

In the hum of conversations and clatter of chairs, two women sat apart, one pouring out years of pain:
A husband who abandoned her.
Five children she couldn't feed.
Debts she couldn't erase.
Prayers she had given up on.

There were no eloquent words in that moment. Just presence. And later, action.

Within two weeks, she and a few friends raised enough money to move Chinny into a dignified apartment. Stocked her pantry. Paid for her kids' school fees. Helped her start a small food business, something she was good at, something that restored her pride.

Chinny was no longer invisible.
She was radiant.

But that wasn't the end of the night.

As she stepped into the cool evening air, exhausted but grateful, she spotted Remi leaning against her car.
Arms folded. Composed as always.
But something in her posture, sagged. .

The lot had mostly emptied, but Remi waited. Not for conversation.
Not for performance.
For rescue.

The writer paused.
Remi looked up and for the first time, her eyes cracked.

"I saw you," Remi said, voice softer than the wind.
"I saw how Chinny smiled today. How Azuka laughed again. How Chuck cried when you spoke life into him."

Then, the mask fell.

"My husband is a serial adulterer," she confessed.
"I smile at church dinners. Host conferences. Raise three children like I'm a fortress, but inside, I'm crumbling."

Tears. Real, shuddering tears.
Not of drama, but of a soul starved for truth.

"I wore control like armor," Remi whispered, voice breaking. "But tonight, when you spoke, my mask slipped."

And in that sacred hush between them, two women stood:
One remembering the girl she once was.
One daring to step into healing.

She reached out, took Remi's trembling hands, and said, "I knew. Because I *was* you. And when the Lord touched me, He didn't just heal me; He gave me new eyes. Every rescue I've stepped into, every hand I've held, they were reflections of the woman I used to be."

And under the hush of the night sky, another door opened.

Remi's sobs broke free, the raw kind that empties the soul only so it can be filled again.
The mask slipped fully.
And another daughter began her rising.

DEVOTIONAL THOUGHT

Healing is not a closed circle.
It's a ripple.

When God rescues you, He gives you the keys to help others find freedom too.
Your testimony becomes the bridge someone else can walk across.
Your scars become a map for the lost.

Your "I made it through" becomes a song that drowns out shame and awakens hope.

And sometimes, the greatest ministry isn't a sermon on a stage;
It's the whisper in a parking lot.
The hand squeezed in a break room.
The moment when your own story tells someone, *"You're not too far gone."*

INTERACTIVE REFLECTION

1. Who in your life might be silently carrying too much?
2. Where have you seen God use your past pain as a bridge for someone else's healing?
3. What simple "yes" could open a door for rescue today?

QUESTION AND ANSWER

Q: What if I feel like I don't have enough to offer?

A: You have more than you think.

Sometimes all you need to offer is your presence. Your empathy. Your story. Your willingness to say, "I see you." God does the multiplying.

SCRIPTURES FOR MEDITATION

- *"The Lord is close to the brokenhearted and saves those who are crushed in spirit."* - **Psalms 34:18 (NIV)**
- *"He comforts us in all our troubles so that we can comfort those in any trouble."* - **2 Corinthians 1:4 (NLT)**
- *"Arise, my love, my beautiful one, and come away."* - **Songs of Solomon 2:10**. *(NKJV)*

REFLECTIVE PROMPTS

- Write about a time when someone's kindness or presence became a rescue for you.
- Ask God today: *Who needs to be seen? Who needs me to notice?*
- Pray for courage to open your heart, even when it feels small.

NOTES FROM MY JOURNAL

I almost missed it, the rescue hidden in plain sight.
I thought healing would end with my own survival.
But it was just the beginning.
God weaves our brokenness into bridges.
Healed people help heal people.

MY REFLECTION NOTES

(Use this space to write your thoughts, prayers, or what stood out to you today.)

_____
_____
_____
_____
_____

Date: _____

Thoughts & Impressions

_____
_____
_____
_____

REFLECTIVE PROMPT

Write down the names of two people you've sensed are silently struggling. Ask God to show you what He wants you to do for them this week.

PRAYER

Lord, thank You for the gift of remembrance. For not letting me forget what pain feels like. So that in another woman's tears, I don't turn away. Let my life be a safe haven for the hurting, a reflection of Your embrace. Use my hands, my voice, my story to build someone else's tomorrow. Amen.

DAY 29

THE STORIES BEHIND THE GLORY

SCRIPTURES

*"You are the light of the world.
A city set on a hill cannot be hidden."*
- Matthew 5:14 (NIV)

*"Arise, shine, for your light has come, and the
glory of the Lord rises upon you."*
- Isaiah 60:1 (NIV)

STORY REFLECTION: THE BEAUTY WE BURY

She had watched them for years, those polished faces on stages, behind glass offices, in the pews, online, on the social media landscape.
Smiling wide. Posting victories. Preaching strength.

But what people rarely told was the story behind their glow.

The hidden bruises. The masks crafted too perfectly.

She saw it most clearly the day she met Candice.

Candice, one of the bank's rising stars.
Sharp as steel. Always impeccable in her pastel suits and muted lipstick.
A woman who commanded rooms without needing to shout.
On social media, she was an emblem of "having it all": career, home, ministry.

But that afternoon in the church lobby, as light filtered softly through stained glass, she saw what others missed.

Candice's hand shook as she reached for her bag.
Her smile faltered at the edges.
And when she finally looked up, the pain behind her designer glasses was too deep to ignore.

Their conversation started innocently enough, "How are you?"
The rehearsed answer came: "I'm fine."
But then, then…………….the pause.

The sacred pause where masks slip if someone is brave enough to stay long enough.

And Candice broke.

She wasn't fine.
Not at all.

Six months earlier, she had been diagnosed with cancer.
The battle was fierce, private, suffocating.
She hid it from everyone outside her inner circle, afraid that vulnerability would cost her influence, pity would steal her power, or worse, that some would whisper that faith should have protected her.

"I thought if I said it out loud, I'd lose everything," Candice whispered.

The writer's heart clenched.
Because wasn't that the lie they all had swallowed at some point? That brokenness disqualifies you. That weakness makes you unworthy.

Candice wept, not just for the sickness, but for the months she had carried it alone under the crushing armor of perfection.

And in that sacred hush, the truth unfolded:
She wasn't the only one hiding.

Most people were.

Some masked debt.
Some masked depression.
Some masked broken marriages.
Some masked illnesses, loneliness, dreams deferred.

We contour our faces until even our pain looks airbrushed.
We photoshop our lives until hope feels filtered.
We curate strength while bleeding silently in private rooms.

And the tragedy is not the pain itself.
It's the silence.
It's pretending.
It's hiding the very testimony that could set someone else free.

She looked at Candice with tears in her own eyes and said,
"You are not less because of your battle. You are more. More real. More radiant."

Because glory without the story intimidates.
But scars shown in the light those heal.

DEVOTIONAL THOUGHT

The world doesn't need another filtered image of success.
It needs the raw, holy truth of scars kissed by grace.

You are not a liability because of your pain.
You are a light because of your survival.

Your battles are not blemishes to hide.
They are bridges for someone else's hope.

God never asked for perfect vessels, only willing ones.
Only open ones.
Only honest ones.

INTERACTIVE REFLECTION

1. What fear has kept you from telling your full story?
2. How might your vulnerability be a bridge to someone else's healing?
3. What testimony have you buried that now needs to rise?

QUESTION AND ANSWER

Q: Will people still respect me if they know my real story?

A: Some might not. But the ones who matter, the ones God sends, will be the ones who find healing because you dared to be real.

SCRIPTURES FOR MEDITATION

- *"We have this treasure in jars of clay."* - **2 Corinthians 4:7. (NKJV).**
- *"They overcame by the blood of the Lamb and the word of their testimony..........-* **Revelation 12:11. (NKJV).**
- *"There is now no condemnation for those who are in Christ Jesus."* - **Romans 8:1. (NKJV).**

REFLECTIVE PROMPTS

- Write a letter to your younger self; what truths do you wish she had known?
- List the parts of your story you once saw as shameful. What do they testify of now?
- Imagine standing before an audience God prepared for you; what would you say if you weren't afraid?

NOTES FROM MY JOURNAL

I thought hiding my wounds would make me whole.
But it's the revealing, the gentle unveiling, that lets the light in.

Scars breathe best in the open air of grace.

> **MY REFLECTION NOTES**
>
> *(Use this space to write your thoughts, prayers, or what stood out to you today.)*
> _____
> _____
> _____
> _____
> _____

Date: _____

Thoughts & Impressions

_____
_____
_____
_____
_____

PRAYER

Father,

Thank You for turning my ashes into beauty, my sorrow into songs.

Teach me not to be ashamed of the battles You helped me survive.

Help me to tell my story, not to boast, but to bear witness.

Let my honesty become a lighthouse in someone else's night.

Let my scars sing of Your faithfulness.

And when fear tempts me to hide again, remind me:

You dwell in the places I once tried to cover.

I am safe to be seen.

Amen.

DAY 30

THE DAY MERCY SPOKE

SCRIPTURES

"The Lord is close to the brokenhearted and saves those who are crushed in spirit."
- Psalm 34:18 (NIV)

"You will seek me and find me when you seek me with all your heart."
- Jeremiah 29:13 (NIV)

STORY REFLECTION: THE ROAD TO REDEMPTION

Azuka sat in the back row of the church, her shoulders slumped, her face a pale reflection of the pain she carried inside. The weight of shame was crushing, and she could feel it, every whisper, every sidelong glance, reminding her of the mistake she had made. Suspended. Exiled from the community she had once been so deeply a part of. Her sin, her failure, was on full display, and the sting of rejection cut deeper than any physical wound.

The murmurs of the crowd didn't help. It wasn't just the suspension; it was the complete ostracization. She could feel their eyes on her, some filled with judgment, others masked with pity. There was no room for grace, only the cold edge of condemnation. And the weight of it all, the whispers, the isolation, the stares, left her feeling like a ghost, unnoticed and unloved.

She had thought about walking away. There had been nights she lay awake, torn between the pain of rejection and the ache of feeling alone in a room full of people. There were even moments, just moments, when the thought of ending it all felt like a way to escape the unbearable weight of shame.

Azuka had once been confident, a passionate young woman who knew God's love deeply. But now, she couldn't remember the last time she had felt close to Him. Her sin, her brokenness, made her feel like an imposter. She no longer recognized herself. She no longer knew where to turn.

That's when I saw her. She was sitting there, small and crumpled in the back, her eyes hollow, looking down as if the very ground might swallow her whole. My heart broke seeing her like that. The woman I had known so full of life, now shrouded in darkness.

I walked toward her, my heart racing as I took the seat next to her. We didn't speak at first. I didn't need to ask her what was wrong; the silence between us spoke volumes. She didn't need more people telling her what she had done wrong. She didn't need more judgment. She needed to know she was seen. She needed to know that in her brokenness, there was still a way back.

Finally, she spoke, her voice trembling, barely a whisper. "I don't know how to come back from this," she said. "I've failed. I've ruined everything. I've lost everything, and I can't bear it anymore."

Her words cracked through the quietness of the church, and I could hear the raw, vulnerable pain in her voice. Azuka wasn't just mourning a failed relationship or a mistake. She was mourning the death of herself, her worth, and her hope.

I gently took her hand, steadying her with my touch. "Azuka," I said softly, my voice firm yet filled with compassion, "you're not beyond God's reach. You are not forsaken."

She shook her head, her tears falling freely now, staining her cheeks. "But............they've rejected me. The church has turned its back on me. How can God still love me? I've fallen so far."

I felt her heart breaking with every word, and I knew in that moment I had to speak truth into her pain. "God's love isn't like theirs, Azuka. His love doesn't leave when we fall. His love doesn't walk away when we mess up. It's unconditional. It's always there, even when we feel we don't deserve it. The church may have suspended you, but God is here with open arms, ready to restore you."

Her sobs softened, but the hurt was still there, deep in her eyes. "But I've been so lost. I don't know how to come back to Him."

I squeezed her hand, my voice firm but tender. "It's not about what you've done, Azuka. It's about the relationship you're willing to rebuild with God. He's not waiting for you to be perfect; He's waiting for you to come back, to seek Him with all your heart. And He will forgive you, because He's the God of second chances."

I leaned in closer, my voice low and earnest. "You may have stumbled, but you haven't fallen out of His reach. Don't let your mistakes keep you from running back to Him. Your healing and restoration aren't about getting it right; they're about a heart that's willing to return. God sees your repentance, He sees your heart, and He loves you enough to walk with you through this."

Azuka looked up at me, a flicker of hope in her eyes. "But what if it's too late?"

I shook my head. "It's never too late. You're not forsaken, Azuka. God is with you, even now, and He will carry you through this."

The rest of the service passed in a blur. Azuka wasn't the same woman who had walked in that day. The weight of shame wasn't gone entirely, but she had made the first step toward grace. Her posture had softened. The burden had been lifted just enough for her to breathe.

DEVOTIONAL THOUGHT

Azuka's story is a reminder that no matter how far we fall, God is always ready to pick us up. We may face rejection, guilt, and the heavy weight of condemnation from others, but God's love remains. His grace is always sufficient, and His arms are always open, ready to welcome us back. Even when we are at our lowest point, feeling like we've been abandoned by all, God is there, never leaving, never forsaking.

Just as Paul wrote about discipline, the goal is restoration, not punishment. The purpose is to bring us back to God, to remind us of His love and to help us find our way again. It's not the church or the crowd that determines our worth; it's God's love that defines us.

INTERACTIVE REFLECTION

1. Have you ever felt so far from God that you thought you couldn't come back? What helped you find your way back?
3. When others have judged you, how have you dealt with their rejection? How can you remind yourself of God's constant love?
4. Who in your life might need to hear that it's never too late to return to God?

QUESTION AND ANSWER

Q: What if I'm so far gone that even God can't help me?

A: No one is beyond God's reach. His forgiveness is limitless, and His love is constant. No matter where you are in life, He is always ready to welcome you back when you turn to Him with a repentant heart.

SCRIPTURES FOR MEDITATION

- *"Let the wicked forsake their ways and the unrighteous their thoughts. Let them turn to the Lord, and He will have mercy on them, and to our God, for He will freely pardon."* - **Isaiah 55:7**. (NKJV)
- *"If we confess our sins, He is faithful and just and will forgive us our sins and purify us from all unrighteousness."* - **1 John 1:9**. (NKJV).
- *"Therefore, there is now no condemnation for those who are in Christ Jesus."* - **Romans 8:1**. (NKJV).

REFLECTIVE PROMPTS

- Write about a time you felt the weight of guilt or shame. How did God meet you at that moment?
- How can you begin to rebuild your relationship with God, even if you've stumbled in the past?
- Who do you need to extend God's grace to today, and how can you do that?

NOTES FROM MY JOURNAL

Azuka's story is a testament to the grace and mercy of God. When we think we're beyond hope, God is there, ready to meet us in our brokenness. His forgiveness is not based on what we've done but on His unchanging love for us. And no matter how far we fall, His arms are always open, waiting to carry us home.

MY REFLECTION NOTES

(Use this space to write your thoughts, prayers, or what stood out to you today.)

_____
_____
_____
_____
_____

Date: _____

Thoughts & Impressions

_____
_____
_____
_____
_____

PRAYER

Heavenly Father,

Thank You for Your unending love and grace. I thank You that, no matter how far we may fall or how heavy our burdens may be, You are always there to lift us up. You see us in our brokenness and draw near to heal us. Lord, help me to remember that Your forgiveness is greater than any shame, and Your love is stronger than any rejection. Teach me to seek You with all my heart and to trust in Your grace when I feel undeserving. I pray for those who are feeling distant from You, that they may know Your open arms, ready to receive them back. May we always remember that we are not forsaken, but cherished by You.

In Jesus' name, Amen.

DAY 31

THE SACRED HUSH

SCRIPTURES

"In quietness and trust is your strength."
- **Isaiah 30:15. (NKJV)**

"I am my beloved's, and His desire is for me."
- **Songs of Solomon 7:10. (NKJV).**

STORY REFLECTION: THE SACRED HUSH

She didn't need to be impressive today.

There was no need for eloquence, no pressure to "show up strong." She wasn't trying to rescue, perform, or explain.

She just sat there still, aware, undone in the most beautiful way.

A hush settled over her, not hollow, not heavy, but holy.
It wrapped itself around her like a weighted blanket of mercy.
She hadn't arrived. She wasn't complete.
But she wasn't hiding anymore either.

She was clay.
Warm. Yielding. Still in the Potter's hand.

There had been days when she thought healing meant reaching a finish line. But here, in the quiet, she knew better.
Healing was a rhythm. A breath. A hush. A whisper of surrender.
And this? This was just another step in the becoming.

She looked out the window, tea cradled between her palms, heart cradled in the presence of God.

She was no longer anxious to "be fixed."
She had learned to simply be... held.

She wasn't Lena. Or Miriam. Or Remi.
She was still herself, flawed, healing, bold in quiet ways.
A woman in progress. A daughter still being written. A vessel still being poured.

And still, He called her **Beloved**.
Still, He whispered, *"You are Mine."*

There would be more doors. More stories. More voices to unmask.

But today wasn't about what came next.
Today was about rest.

Not the kind that says "I'm finished."
But the kind that says, *"Even here, I'm seen. Even now, I'm loved."*

This wasn't the end.
This was the hush before the next unveiling.
The pause before the crescendo.
The breath before the rise.

DEVOTIONAL THOUGHT

Sometimes, healing doesn't roar; it whispers.

We wait for the thunder, but it's in the hush where God often moves most deeply.

Healing is not a finish line; it's a rhythm of surrender.

You are not behind if you're still breaking.
You are not less holy because you're still growing.
You are not disqualified because you're not yet whole.

You are clay, beloved in the becoming.

And God does His best work in quiet places.

Let this be your sacred hush:
Not silence from pain, but stillness in purpose.

Day 31 isn't a conclusion. It's an invitation. An invitation into quiet confidence. Into stillness that strengthens. Into a rhythm where identity isn't tied to exhaustion, and worth isn't bound to performance.

This is your sacred hush. This is where the healing lingers.

Let it be holy.

INTERACTIVE REFLECTION

1. What does "quiet confidence" mean to you today?
2. Have you ever mistaken stillness for stagnation?
3. Where in your life can you pause, not to retreat, but to rest and listen?

QUESTION AND ANSWER

Q: Does the journey end now that I'm no longer broken?

A: No. The journey simply shifts. From healing to wholeness. From survival to surrender. From silence to song. You are still becoming and you are already beloved.

SCRIPTURES FOR MEDITATION

- *"We are the clay. You are the potter; we are all the work of Your hand."* - **Isaiah 64:8. (NKJV)**
- *"I have calmed and quieted my soul……………"* - **Psalms 131:2. (NKJV)**
- *"He will quiet you with His love."* - **Zephaniah 3:17. (;NKJV).**

- *"You who dwell in the gardens with friends in attendance, let me hear your voice!"* - **Songs of Solomon 8:13. (ESV)**
- *"For anyone who enters God's rest also rests from their works............ "* - **Hebrews 4:10. (NKJV)**.

REFLECTIVE PROMPTS

- What would it look like to embrace stillness this week?
- Write down the things you no longer have to perform for.
- List three ways God has met you in quiet moments.

NOTES FROM MY JOURNAL

I'm not there yet.
I haven't figured it all out.
I still flinch, ache and wonder.
But I'm held.
And maybe- just maybe, that's what healing really is.
Being held in the hush.

MY REFLECTION NOTES

(Use this space to write your thoughts, prayers, or what stood out to you today.)

_____
_____
_____
_____
_____

Date: _____

Thoughts & Impressions

_____
_____
_____
_____
_____

PRAYER

Father, Thank You for the hush. For the sacred stillness that reminds me I am more than what I've done, more than who I've rescued, more than the pain I've endured.

Thank You for every door You opened, every person You let me meet, every story You allowed me to hold. But most of all, thank You for staying.

As I rest here, on this final day of Volume One, I don't say goodbye. I say: I'm ready. Ready for what's next. Ready to listen. Ready to rise.

In the quiet, I am Yours.

Amen.

FINAL WHISPER

You've walked the long hallway.
Touched every crack in the wall.
Learned to love even the silence.
But child,
There are still rooms you haven't entered.
Still doors only *you* can open.
Still stories only *your* scars can unlock.
Volume I was never the destination.
It was only the key.
Volume II?
Heaven already wrote the title.
You're about to live it.
Each of these stories, each door, opened because someone who had once worn the mask dared to look back and see another.
Every rescue was a mirror of her former self. And in every hand she held, she found fragments of the healing still blooming within her.

BACK COVER - THE MASK SHE WORE: THE REBIRTH

She looked like she had it all together.
But under the smile was exhaustion.
Under the laughter, pain.
Behind the strength, a mask.

This is not just another devotional.
This is a journey for the woman who has mastered survival, but forgotten how to breathe.
For the one who shows up for everyone else, but silently wonders if anyone sees *her*.
For the woman who wears the mask so well, it almost became her face.

In these 31 days of raw, story-woven devotion, you'll walk beside a woman who dared to let her mask slip.
And as she sees herself, finally, she begins to see others.
Each door she opens, each hand she holds, becomes a mirror…
A rescue.
A reminder that healing flows not just from being seen but from *seeing others* through healed eyes.

You'll cry. You'll whisper, "That's me."
You'll find sacred silence and truth in every page.
And maybe, just maybe, you'll let your own mask slip too.

This is the sacred hush.
This is your unveiling.
This is where freedom begins.

She wore a mask, but don't be fooled.
It wasn't to hide the pain.
It was to protect the *world* from her fire.

Behind those perfect smiles and perfect posts, she was something else entirely.

A quiet storm in a land of sunshine.

The kind of woman who knew how to wear her grief like it was fashionable.

She made it look easy, effortlessly blending in with the crowd while the world never saw her breaking.

They had no idea that when the mask finally fell, it wouldn't be to expose weakness; it would be to reveal a *warrior*.

You see, the thing about wearing a mask is it doesn't just protect you. It hides the truth from others. Yes. But it also hides the truth from *yourself*.

And now?

Now, she's ready to step into the light, no longer hiding behind the walls she built.

But here's the twist:

They might just be more afraid of who she *really* is than the mask she wore.

So, here's a question! When she lifts the veil, will you be ready for what's underneath?

TEASER VOLUME 2: THE SACRED HUSH

They didn't believe she wrote it.
"Not *her*," they hissed.
"Too plain. Too quiet. Too………….., older."
But she did.
Every word, carved from the rubble they left her in.

The moment the book dropped, so did jaws.
Whispers flew like pigeons in a cathedral:
"She's airing the secrets."
"She's bitter."
"She's brave."
"She's back."

Some saints clutched pearls.
Some sinners lit candles.
The rest? Just watched, mouths open, as the woman they boxed up came with keys.

They tried to shame her with her age.
She built altars with it.
They tried to drown her with the past.
She bottled the flood and called it perfume.

Now doors open where walls used to be.
Now her scars testify louder than sermons.
She's not writing revenge.
She's writing resurrection.

Volume 2 is not for the faint.
It's for the ones who *remember*
And those who *never thought she would.*

www.ingramcontent.com/pod-product-compliance
Lightning Source LLC
Chambersburg PA
CBHW051926160426
43198CB00012B/2053